"*Surviving the Emotional Roller Coaster* is a practical guide modified to provide relevant information for teenagers coping with managing their emotions in today's unusually demanding world. Practicing and using the techniques described in this book affects the ability to regulate emotions, shape a sense of self, and healthy emotional development. I would venture to say that this book is a must-read for all teenagers and those around them."

> —**Rennet Wong-Gates, MSW, RSW**, child, youth, and family therapist

"This excellent resource is filled with great examples and practice exercises that teens can relate to. Van Dijk emphasizes the importance of learning and practicing skills at one's own pace with the goal of making life changes to reduce suffering associated with escalating emotions."

> —**Francine Brill, MD, FRCP(C)**, child and adolescent psychiatrist in private practice in Newmarket, Ontario, Canada, and consultant to New Path Youth and Family Services

D0556337

"Sheri Van Dijk has hit it out of the amusement park with this skill-based approach to surviving the emotional roller coaster. She effectively helps her readers to identify their overwhelming emotions and their behavioral challenges while equipping them with practical strategies to successfully manage them. This clear, step-by-step description of dialectical behavior therapy (DBT) skills will indisputably help teens to navigate the twists and turns of their emotional journey. I will definitely recommend this engaging, easy-to-use manual to my clients and their families, and I will keep it close by as a guide in helping my teen clients to traverse their social and emotional challenges."

—**Francine Mendelowitz, LCSW**, psychotherapist and founder of InterACT New York, an interactive approach to tackling teen challenges

"Sheri Van Dijk has written an accessible workbook that includes useful exercises and relevant examples to help young people grow their knowledge and skills in managing their painful emotions. I will recommend this book to my adolescent clients and parents who consult me."

> —**Karma Guindon, MSW, PhD (candidate), RSW, RMFT**, therapist in private practice, and lecturer at the University of Waterloo

"Surviving the Emotional Roller Coaster is an invaluable resource to any teen, parent, or professional who is dealing with the complex nature of emotional dysregulation. Sheri Van Dijk has found an eloquent and understandable way of explaining comprehensive dialectical behavioral therapy (DBT) concepts to an audience that will greatly benefit. As a clinician, I plan to refer to and draw from her book in my daily practice."

> —**Wendy Hofmann, MSW, RSW**, clinical social worker, and partner at Hofmann & Isaac Individual and Family Counselling in Aurora, Ontario, Canada

"This skill-based book brings together an array of dialectical behavioral therapy (DBT)-based strategies in a well laid out, uniquely easy-to-read fashion. *Surviving the Emotional Roller Coaster* is a must-read as it conveys hope and encouragement to a population that has typically been seen as a clinical challenge. This resource gives readers a practical treatment plan which will undoubtedly lead them on a road to wellness."

> —**Michael Isaac, MEd, RSW**, clinical social worker, and partner at Hofmann & Isaac Individual and Family Counselling in Aurora, Ontario, Canada

"In *Surviving the Emotional Roller Coaster*, Sheri Van Dijk has again written an engaging and user-friendly book. For teens whose emotions make their life feel as if they are on a roller coaster, this book provides hope as Van Dijk has explained the skills of dialectical behavior therapy (DBT) in an understandable and easy-to-follow manner. There are plenty of examples and exercises making this an interactive book. I would definitely recommend this book to clients both young and older."

> —**Marilyn Becker, MSW, RSW**, dialectical behavior therapy (DBT) skills therapist in private practice in Richmond Hill, Ontario, Canada

"*Surviving the Emotional Roller Coaster* is a remarkably helpful resource for teenagers and parents, and practitioners working with teenagers. Sheri Van Dijk's user-friendly workbook offers valuable knowledge and practical skills to help teenagers gain an understanding and awareness of their emotions and learn to manage difficult emotions, and provides guidance to surviving crises with calm. She has done a wonderful job at providing simple practices to help teenagers effectively deal with challenges in their relationships."

> —**Zainib Abdullah, MSW, RSW**, mental health therapist and crisis worker at Southlake Regional Health Centre

the *instant* help solutions series

Young people today need mental health resources more than ever. That's why New Harbinger created the **Instant Help Solutions Series** especially for teens. Written by leading psychologists, physicians, and professionals, these evidence-based self-help books offer practical tips and strategies for dealing with a variety of mental health issues and life challenges teens face, such as depression, anxiety, bullying, eating disorders, trauma, and self-esteem problems.

Studies have shown that young people who learn healthy coping skills early on are better able to navigate problems later in life. Engaging and easy-to-use, these books provide teens with the tools they need to thrive—at home, at school, and on into adulthood.

This series is part of the **New Harbinger Instant Help Books** imprint, founded by renowned child psychologist Lawrence Shapiro. For a complete list of books in this series, visit newharbinger.com.

surviving the emotional roller coaster

dbt skills to help teens manage emotions

SHERI VAN DIJK, MSW

Instant Help Books
An Imprint of New Harbinger Publications, Inc.

Publisher's Note

This publication is designed to provide accurate and authoritative information in regard to the subject matter covered. It is sold with the understanding that the publisher is not engaged in rendering psychological, financial, legal, or other professional services. If expert assistance or counseling is needed, the services of a competent professional should be sought.

Distributed in Canada by Raincoast Books

Copyright © 2016 by Sheri Van Dijk
          Instant Help
          An imprint of New Harbinger Publications, Inc.
          5674 Shattuck Avenue
          Oakland, CA 94609
          www.newharbinger.com

Cover design by Amy Shoup
Acquired by Tesilya Hanauer
Edited by Karen Schader

Library of Congress Cataloging-in-Publication Data

Van Dijk, Sheri, author.
  Surviving the emotional roller coaster : DBT skills to help teens manage emotions / Sheri Van Dijk, MSW.
      pages cm. -- (The instant help solutions series)
  ISBN 978-1-62625-240-0 (pbk. : alk. paper) -- ISBN 978-1-62625-241-7 (pdf e-book) -- ISBN 978-1-62625-242-4 (epub) 1. Emotions in adolescence--Juvenile literature. 2. Dialectical behavior therapy--Juvenile literature. I. Title.
  BF724.3.E5V363 2016
  155.5'124--dc23

                              2015032491

Printed in the United States of America

18   17   16

10   9   8   7   6   5   4   3   2   1   First printing

Contents

Introduction

If this book has caught your eye, chances are you know all too
well about the emotional roller coaster—and you know that it's
not a fun ride. In fact, it can be quite painful and scary (not in
a good way) and can lead to a lot of other difficulties in your
life, including mood problems like depression and anxiety, or
complications in relationships. In turn, these issues can lead to
problematic behaviors like self-harm, substance abuse, eating
disorders, or aggression toward others. If any of these things
sound familiar, this book is for you; it will help you survive
the roller coaster and teach you skills to help you manage your
emotions so that you're in control of your life, rather than just
being a passenger along for the ride. Of course, the skills in this
book can also help you not climb aboard the roller coaster to
begin with!

Emotional Pain: Typical or Overwhelming?

Unfortunately, emotional pain is part of life; there's no avoiding it. Someone leaves us and we feel hurt or afraid. We don't get something we really want and we feel sad or angry. Someone dies and we feel grief, loss, and loneliness. Most of us understand that these experiences are normal—that the hurt, disappointment, anger, sadness, and so on are unavoidable. Most people know that emotional pain is just that—painful—but like all pain, it will pass. Most people can understand why they feel the way they do, and so they can allow themselves to experience whatever they're feeling and gradually move on.

For some, emotional pain is overwhelming and all-consuming. It is triggered by things other people wouldn't typically react to and is so intense that they can't even think straight. Their emotions feel intolerable and unbearable, as if the pain will go on forever. Their emotional reaction is higher than what would typically be seen as warranted by the situation, and it takes them longer to come back down from that intense emotion to their usual selves. Understanding their emotions is unthinkable, and all they want to do is avoid the experience. These people have *emotion dysregulation*.

What Causes Emotion Dysregulation?

Research continues in the field of mental health, and while there are theories about why mental illness develops, the bottom line is that we still don't really understand why some people develop mental health problems and others don't. But in *dialectical behavior therapy*—the treatment I use and will soon explain more about—the *biosocial theory* explains the development of emotion regulation problems as stemming from two things: biology and environment.

Biology

According to the biosocial theory, some people are born with a higher likelihood of developing emotion regulation problems. Genetics is one reason people might be born this way. Just as I was born with hazel eyes, some people are born more sensitive than others. A second reason is that a traumatic experience can affect the human brain in such a way as to make a person more emotionally vulnerable. And a third reason is mental illness: a person who has a mental health problem such as a mood or anxiety disorder, especially if it's not well managed by available treatments, will have more problems regulating emotions.

Environment

The second part to this theory is the environment a person grows up in. It's important to understand that someone could be born more highly sensitive and not go on to develop problems in life, and be able to manage emotions relatively well. But, according to the biosocial theory, when you put a highly sensitive person in an environment that is pervasively invalidating, problems will arise. A *pervasively invalidating environment* is one in which a person regularly receives the message that there's something wrong or inaccurate about her internal experience; for example, she might be told that she shouldn't feel the way she's feeling or given the message that her opinions or beliefs are "wrong." Perhaps she's punished for her feeling, or her feeling is ignored.

Most people experience this kind of invalidation at times—unfortunately, we don't always feel understood by others! The key here is that the invalidation is happening regularly. The other piece to remember is that many people might experience this kind of invalidation on a regular basis, but it's the combination of being a highly sensitive person and being in this kind of environment that will fairly inevitably lead to problems with emotion regulation.

However, often people are invalidating without meaning to be. Your mom doesn't understand why you're so angry with yourself about the B you got on your report card, and the message you get from her is that you shouldn't feel this way. Or your best friend tells you that she's tired of having to put up with your explosions of anger and needs a break from you. Or your parents make you go to their work holiday party and then get angry with you when you're so anxious that you feel sick to your stomach and they have to leave the party early. You can see that, in these situations, people probably aren't trying to be hurtful; they simply can't understand your emotional reaction, even though they might be trying to.

Finally, I want to point out that, for the most part, we're not looking to blame anyone here. Sometimes there is blame to be placed: no one should be sexually, physically, emotionally, or verbally abused or neglected. If this is happening to you, I hope you'll read these words and understand that this situation is not acceptable. Please seek help. Talk to a family member, a teacher, a religious leader, a friend's parent, or someone else you feel you can trust, and let that person know what's happening so he or she can help get you out of your abusive environment.

So this theory isn't about placing blame. It's just about helping you see why you are the way you are. This recognition can help you stop blaming yourself, because you didn't put yourself in this position—it's a combination of your genetics and your environment.

Effects of Emotion Dysregulation

If you're relating to what I've described as emotion dysregulation, you already know what kinds of problems it causes in your life, but let's take a look at a few situations connected to difficulties managing your emotions, ones that you might be able to identify with.

Not Knowing Who You Are

If you're a highly sensitive person growing up in an invalidating environment, you may have gotten so used to being invalidated that you actually start to do it to yourself. In other words, you tell yourself you "shouldn't" be feeling the way you are, or perhaps you look to the people around you to see how you "should" be feeling. When you do this often enough, you may actually stop being aware of the emotions you feel, and the beliefs and opinions you hold. You're so busy trying to not be invalidated by others that you put your true self aside and try to be what others want you to be (or at least who you think they want you to be). In the end, you don't really know who this person you call "me" is.

Problems in Relationships

If you're highly sensitive, it's often very difficult for others to understand why you react to things the way you do. (Let's face it, it's probably often difficult for *you* to understand why you react to things the way you do!) Even when people are trying to understand and clearly still don't get where you're coming from, you're left feeling different, like you don't belong or fit in. So you might feel not only lonely but also angry at others for not understanding you. How many times have you gotten so angry at another person that either you exploded at her and ended the relationship yourself, or she ended the relationship because of the way you treated her? Often people with emotion regulation problems lose relationships because their emotions get in the way.

Unhealthy or Destructive Behaviors

When people don't know how to manage emotions, they sometimes end up turning to unhealthy or even destructive behaviors in an attempt to cope. This can result in a number of problem behaviors, including but not limited to the following: using or abusing drugs and alcohol; escaping by gaming or gambling; turning to disordered eating such as overeating, bingeing, or refusing to eat; self-harm (for example, cutting yourself); engaging in dangerous sexual practices like having unprotected sex, or having sex with multiple partners; or thinking about or engaging in suicidal behaviors.

Because you haven't yet learned what to do with intense emotions, and because your emotions get so intense much of the time, it makes sense you'd turn to these problem behaviors;

and of course we don't want you to continue with these behaviors, which can have so many negative consequences. This is where dialectical behavior therapy comes in.

What Is Dialectical Behavior Therapy?

Dialectical behavior therapy (DBT), a treatment developed by psychologist Marsha Linehan, teaches people skills to help them manage their emotions more effectively so that they're happier and healthier, and so that their lives are closer to the way they'd like them to be.

These DBT skills are separated into four groups:

* Mindfulness skills

  Mindfulness skills have you practicing staying in the present moment (as opposed to living in the past or the future) and being more accepting of your present experience (rather than judging everything, which increases your painful emotions). These skills will help you get to know yourself better, as you'll be paying more attention to your internal experience and accepting it rather than invalidating it, and also help you reduce the amount of emotional pain you're experiencing on a daily basis.

* Distress tolerance skills

  Distress tolerance skills are geared toward helping you get through crisis situations without making things worse by engaging in some of the problem behaviors mentioned earlier.

✳ Interpersonal effectiveness skills

Interpersonal effectiveness is about how to be more effective in the relationships in your life, and with people in a more general sense. When you can increase your effectiveness in this area and improve your relationships, you'll often find that it's easier to deal with emotions as they arise.

✳ Emotion regulation skills

Emotion regulation skills help you learn to identify your emotions more effectively and to be more accepting of those emotions, recognizing that although they're often painful or uncomfortable, they serve a purpose and you need them. Sometimes these skills will help you reduce the intensity of an emotion, and sometimes they will help you change an emotion, but the overall theme of these skills is working on accepting your emotional experience and learning to bear the pain more skillfully, to tolerate the experience instead of trying to get rid of it.

While emotion regulation skills are central to what you're trying to accomplish, I left them until last because really, all the skills in this book are going to help you manage your emotions more effectively: When you're living in the present moment and are more accepting, you'll have fewer and less intense emotions, making them easier to manage. When you're dealing with crisis situations more effectively, you'll feel better about yourself and will have more support from the people in your life, making

emotions easier to manage. And when you're being more effective in your relationships, they will go more smoothly and
will lead to less drama in your life, making emotions easier to
manage!

Hopefully you're beginning to see that these skills are really
going to help. But in order for you to get the most out of the
skills, we need to look at how you can get the most out of this
book.

Your Next Steps

If you have absolutely no intention of working to make changes
in your life, save yourself some time and put this book back
on the shelf. Like most other therapies, DBT is not about just
reading a book and hoping for the best. You can't even expect
that if you read this book and do a bit of practice for a while,
things will get better. Nope, this treatment is about making life
changes. If you're willing to take the time to read this book and
put in the work to practice what you're going to learn in these
pages, I guarantee that you'll see a positive change—even if it's
just a tiny one at first. And the longer you practice, the better
things will get. Let me tell you a story…

As a teenager, Marsha Linehan was hospitalized for over
two years because of mental illness. She would cut herself, burn
herself, and pound her head against the floor and the walls.
She had borderline personality disorder. As an adult, Dr. Linehan created DBT out of the skills, tools, and techniques she had
learned to heal herself.

So don't you dare think you can't do this. Things may be really, really difficult for you right now—and you *can* make them better. I really hope that you're still with me, and that you can have the courage that Dr. Linehan had to turn the page and start learning.

Chapter 1

Mindfulness: Waking Up to Your Life

You might be thinking *Waking up? I'm already awake!* You might be wondering how on earth you could go through life not awake, but the truth is that many people do. They go through life not fully aware of what's happening in the present moment, not fully aware of what they're thinking or feeling, or even how they're behaving. That's what this chapter is about: you're going to learn about a technique called *mindfulness*, which is going to help you become more aware of yourself, and which, over time, will help you wake up to your life.

By the way, you may be thinking your problem is that you're already too awake, that you're too aware of your emotions, for example, and this is what makes them so painful. If this is the case, I suggest that you still need to work on waking up—to the world around you. You'll learn skills to help with both of these problems throughout this book.

What Is Mindfulness?

Mindfulness is the core skill in DBT, precisely because it helps you wake up to your life. You can't change something until you first become aware of, or wake up to, what the reality is—of yourself, of your reactions to others, of the effect you have on others, of what's going on around you, and so on.

Mindfulness is about doing one thing at a time, in the present moment, with your full attention, and with acceptance. So think of this skill as having two parts: first, focusing on the one task or activity you're doing in the here and now, in just this one moment; and second, accepting whatever you happen to find in this moment.

Focusing on the Present Moment

How often do you find yourself thinking about anything but what you're doing in the present? Maybe you're doing your homework, and instead of really focusing on your assignment, you're thinking about your plans for this weekend, or the fight you had with your parents, or what you'll buy your girlfriend for your upcoming anniversary, or anything else. You might be partly thinking about what you're doing, but your full attention isn't in the present; it's everywhere else! Sound familiar? Or maybe you're walking home from school, and instead of focusing on the walk and on the environment around you, you're thinking about all the homework you have to do later, or the college applications you have to fill out, or how hard the SATs are going to be. Again, you're not focusing on the one thing you're doing right now—walking. Instead, your mind is wandering to many other things.

When you're being mindful, you bring your attention back over and over again to what you're doing in this moment. So when you're doing your homework and your attention wanders to your plans for this weekend, you notice that you've wandered, and you bring your attention back. Each time you wander, you do your best to notice it and continue to bring your attention back to whatever you're doing in this moment.

Of course, some things are easier to focus on than others. You might not find that your mind wanders much when you're watching your favorite TV show, reading a really good book, or playing your guitar. Some things will hold your attention more easily, just as some things will be really difficult for you to stay focused on—like maybe your homework! Regardless of how difficult or easy it is, though, it will be to your benefit to keep bringing your attention back to just this moment. We'll look more at the why momentarily. First, let's look at the second part to this skill: acceptance.

Accepting the Present Moment

Have you ever noticed how judgmental you are? And I don't mean that as a judgment! For most of us, it's just a fact: we *are* judgmental creatures. So that makes this part of mindfulness pretty tough, and in fact, it's so difficult that we're going to address this as a skill all on its own in chapter 4. For now, though, you need to have a bit of an idea of how to practice acceptance as part of mindfulness.

Let's go back to some of our previous examples. Let's say you're working on your homework assignment, and your little sister is making a whole lot of noise in the next room. Chances are, you're judging her: *What's the matter with her? Doesn't she know I'm working?* Or *She's so annoying! She shouldn't be so loud.* Or *Mom or Dad should be telling her to be quiet!* These are all judgments.

With mindfulness, the idea is that you're focusing on what you're doing in this moment, and you're practicing being accepting of whatever is in the moment. Whether it's noise or other outside distractions, or your own thoughts, emotions, or physical sensations, you practice being nonjudgmental. So with your sister, acceptance might look something like this: *She's being really loud; I'm distracted by the noise* or *It's hard for me to concentrate when my sister's making so much noise.* No judgments—you're just sticking to the facts. Again, we'll come back to this idea later, so don't worry if it doesn't make perfect sense just yet.

Now, let's look at why I'm teaching you this skill and how it's going to help you in the long run.

How Mindfulness Will Help You Survive the Emotional Roller Coaster

Once you start practicing mindfulness, you'll find that the world will no longer be passing you by and you'll be more aware of yourself: the thoughts you're thinking, the physical sensations in your body, the emotions you're feeling. You'll also be more aware of what's going on around you; you'll be participating, involved, and engaged in life. I'm going to break this down a little further so you really understand some of the many ways that mindfulness will be helpful.

Reducing Emotional Pain

Do you think you spend a lot of time thinking about the past? It might be the distant past—things you've done, or things that happened to you. Or it might be the more recent past—the argument you had with your parents the other day, or the grade you got on an exam. If you do spend a lot of time in the past, think for a moment about the emotions that tend to come up when you're there. Anger? Resentment? Frustration? Regret? Sadness? Sometimes you might find that you go to pleasant memories, like the fun you had with your friends last weekend or when you were on vacation with your family over the summer. But for the most part, we tend not to go to happy places; instead, we go to the painful memories.

On the flip side, do you think you spend a lot of time thinking about the future? Worrying about whether you'll get into the college you want to go to; feeling nervous about whether the girl you like will say yes if you ask her to prom; feeling anxious about making a fool of yourself if you go to the big party this weekend, and so on. Does this sound like you? Again, sometimes when we think of the future we have pleasant emotions. Maybe you daydream about the trip to Costa Rica that's booked for January, or you think about how great it's going to be when you graduate from high school and go to college. But most of the time, instead of thinking about the pleasant things, we're focusing on the negative, and this generates anxiety and worry.

Hopefully you can see the theme here: when you're not living in the present moment, there's more emotional pain. Of course, the present isn't always pleasant either. But if you're being more mindful, even when there's pain in the present there's still less pain, because you're dealing only with the pain of the present, rather than the pain of the present, past, and future all at the same time.

Acceptance, the other part of mindfulness, also reduces the amount of emotional pain in your life. Again, as you'll see when we discuss this further in chapter 4, judgments actually increase your emotional pain. So when you're being more mindful, you're more accepting, which means less pain.

Increasing Positive Emotions

So far we've been focusing on how mindfulness will help reduce painful emotions; but just as important, when you're being more mindful and waking up to your life, you'll be in the present moment more often to notice when positive things are happening. Picture this: You're at your prom. You asked the girl you like to go with you and she said yes, but now she's socializing with other people instead of just sitting with you. So you start to worry that she doesn't really like you; maybe she agreed to come with you only because no one else asked her. You might start to worry, for example, that she's going to ditch you and you're going to look like an idiot. What happens in this scenario? Well, you probably aren't having a very good time. You might miss out on some good music because you're so caught up in your thoughts that you don't even notice what they're playing. You're probably missing out on some good times with your friends. Maybe you would normally dance, but you feel too anxious to get yourself moving so you stay in your chair, which, of course, might have other consequences—maybe your date would have come to dance with you if you'd gotten up, but you missed out on that opportunity because you were too caught up in your worries.

As difficult as it can be at times, when you can be mindful and focus on the present moment, you'll find that you notice the positives more. So if you kept turning your attention away from those worry thoughts, you might have heard someone at your table talking about how much he loves motorcycles, and you could have had a great conversation about bikes, which is one of your passions. Or you would have heard the joke that one of your friends told, which might have made you smile for a moment. Or you would have enjoyed the music more...

There are often small positive experiences that take place around you that you probably miss out on because you're so caught up in your thoughts. This is what waking up to your life is about.

Feeling Calm and Relaxed

Mindfulness can sometimes help you feel more relaxed and calm. But while this can be a beneficial side effect, it isn't actually the goal of mindfulness. The only goals of mindfulness are to be in the present moment and to be more accepting. And sometimes, you might be practicing mindfulness and there's no way you're going to feel relaxed and calm. Let's say you have to do a presentation in class, and public speaking makes you anxious. You could practice mindfulness—noticing that your heart is pounding and your palms are sweaty, noticing that you're having worry thoughts about making a fool of yourself or that you're going to forget your speech. You're focusing on the present moment, you're accepting it...and there's *still* no way you'll feel relaxed in that moment! The alternative, of course—not practicing mindfulness—often increases the painful emotions you're experiencing, because you continue to think the worst about what might happen and because you're not accepting the experience but fighting it instead, which increases your emotional pain. So mindfulness is not about relaxation.

But think about it: When you're in the present moment more often, instead of caught up in thoughts about everything in your head, you'll probably feel less overwhelmed. When you're accepting your experience instead of judging it and fighting it, you'll probably feel more at peace. When you're doing one activity at a time instead of three, you're going to be less scattered and more focused. The other part to this is that often the activities you choose to do mindfully are activities that help you feel calm and relaxed; for example, reading a book, watching TV, petting your dog, lying in the bathtub, taking a walk, or sitting outside.

Increasing Self-Control

I've already mentioned that when you're being mindful you're more aware of your thoughts, physical sensations, and emotions. When you can increase your awareness of something, you open up more choices for yourself—again, you wake up to your life. So often people go through life on automatic pilot, just allowing thoughts and emotions to take them along for the ride. And they do this because they've never really learned that they can take control; that they can be in the driver's seat and direct where they want to go and what they want to think about.

When you're living your life more mindfully, and you're more aware of what's going on inside of you, you can choose whether you want to continue down that road. So when you're sitting at prom watching your date mingle, and you notice your thoughts start to turn in the painful direction of worry and anxiety, you now have a choice: do you allow your thoughts to continue down that path, or do you get up and do something to prevent this—like maybe grab your date and take her to the dance floor?

Improving Concentration and Memory

People often have difficulty concentrating, especially if there's an additional problem like attention deficit/hyperactivity disorder (ADHD), or even something like depression or anxiety. The skill of mindfulness has you practicing concentration. Bringing your attention back to the present, often over and over again, exercises the concentration muscles in your brain. Over time, your ability to focus will improve.

When you're more able to focus on something, you'll have a better memory for it later. Have you ever walked home from school and not had a memory of at least some of the walk? Nowadays with our dependence on smartphones, this kind of thing happens a lot. Your mom pokes her head into your bedroom and is having a conversation with you; you're half listening, but at the same time you're texting your friend or browsing your Facebook newsfeed. Do you really remember the conversation you just had with your mom? Probably not, because you weren't really focusing on it. When your attention is divided, you won't have a good memory for what you've been doing. If you're practicing mindfulness, you're intentionally doing just one thing in the moment—so when your mom wants to talk to you, you put your phone down, or you ask her to wait a second while you finish sending your text, and then you turn your full attention to the conversation. When you're concentrating on just that one thing, you're going to remember it later, so mindfulness will also help improve your memory.

Finding Balance

Since the goal of this book is to help you survive the emotional roller coaster, finding *balance* probably sounds like a pretty good idea, right? Mindfulness helps us develop something called equanimity, or balance—basically, an evenness or stability in our state of mind, even when situations are causing us stress or other emotional pain. This doesn't mean that we don't react to things; it means that we don't let our reactions overtake us. In other words, we still feel emotions when situations arise, but we are able to access our inner wisdom and view the situation objectively, which helps us prevent ourselves from being overcome by the emotion and acting in ways we later regret. When you're practicing mindfulness regularly, you develop this sense of balance, so that even when life becomes painful, you maintain the ability to choose how to respond, rather than simply reacting from your emotions.

Hopefully by now you're seeing the many ways in which mindfulness can be helpful for you. So let's look at how exactly to practice mindfulness.

How to Practice Mindfulness

First and foremost, it's important to remember that you can do absolutely anything mindfully—you can breathe, eat, have conversations with people, do your homework, shower, get dressed...the list is literally endless. And it's also important to recognize that the expectation is not that you practice mindfulness 24/7. While the goal is to live your life more mindfully, constantly being mindful isn't realistic; and we also know that allowing our minds to float and daydream increases creativity, which of course we don't want to get in the way of!

Many of the skills you'll read about in this book are about finding balance, and mindfulness is no different. You'll want to practice regularly so that this skill is accessible when you want it and need it, but don't pressure yourself to do it constantly. Rather, think of yourself as setting out on a path; you're never going to get to the end of the path, and that's not the point. The point is the journey, and that is mindfulness.

Four Steps to Mindfulness

So far we've talked about many of the things you can do mindfully and the benefits of practicing, and we've looked at how not being mindful keeps you stuck on the emotional roller coaster. To make things easier, let's break mindfulness down into steps, so you can see exactly how you can bring mindfulness to anything in your life.

1. Pick an activity.

   Remember, you can do anything mindfully, so pick an activity to focus on and bring your intention to that activity. If you're going to read, you may decide to read one page mindfully; if you're walking your dog, you might choose to walk mindfully from your front door to the end of the street...

2. Pay attention.

Bring your attention to doing that one activity in the present moment. While you read, just focus on the words you're reading and becoming involved in the story. While you walk, you might notice how it feels to walk physically—such as the feeling of your feet on the sidewalk—or you might choose to notice the environment around you; for example, a squirrel that runs across the road, or the trees at the side of the road.

3. Notice when you wander.

Our brains generate thousands of thoughts every day, so it's almost impossible for your mind not to wander. Notice this; acknowledge it.

4. Come back to the present.

Bring your attention back to the activity you're doing in the here and now, without judging. This means that you don't judge yourself for wandering and that you don't judge whatever else happens to come into your awareness; for example, an emotion that arises within you, a certain thought that comes to mind, or something you experience with your senses. Whatever you happen to notice, just observe it instead of judging it.

And then you continue doing steps 3 and 4 over and over and over again: you notice your attention wander, and you gently (without judging) bring yourself back; you wander again, and you bring yourself back again. This is mindfulness. It's not about staying in the present, but about noticing when you're no longer there and returning to that moment.

Now let's put this into practice, starting with what we call an *informal practice*—where you're doing something you would be doing anyway, and you bring mindfulness to that activity. These are things like brushing your teeth or having conversations with people.

Exercise: Informal Mindfulness Practice

Choose something right now. It might be reading the rest of this page, or you might want to stop reading for a moment and make some notes about what you've read so far, or you might decide you need to take a bit of a break from reading and go watch TV or listen to some music for a few minutes. Pick an activity (step 1), and bring mindfulness to it: start to focus on that activity (step 2); notice when your attention wanders (step 3); and as best as you can without judging yourself or anything about your experience, bring your attention back to that activity (step 4). You might stay focused for a few seconds or a minute before you wander again; just notice that (step 3), and without judging, return your attention to the task (step 4).

Informal practices such as these help you live your life more mindfully. When you're bringing mindfulness to a variety of activities and tasks throughout the day, you're living your life more in the present moment and with acceptance, which over time helps increase your sense of equanimity, or balance.

In a *formal practice*, you have to set aside some time to practice something mindfully, such as a breathing exercise or a body scan. This kind of exercise is also referred to as *mindfulness meditation*, but it's not about clearing your mind or sitting cross-legged on the floor chanting to yourself. Rather, it's what we've already been talking about: noticing your experience and practicing being accepting of it, whatever it is. Take a look at the following formal practice; you might want to read it through once and then practice it on your own as best as you can.

Exercise: Formal Mindfulness Practice with the Breath

Sitting comfortably, turn your attention to your breathing. You don't have to change your breathing in any way; just notice how it feels to breathe. Notice the feel of the air as it passes through your nostrils; feel your lungs expand and contract as you breathe in and out; just notice whatever there is to notice about breathing. At some point, you'll notice that your attention has wandered—perhaps you hear your parents coming in the door downstairs; maybe your stomach growls and you start to think about what you'll have for dinner; or maybe nothing in particular distracts you, and you're just off day-dreaming as we do sometimes. Whatever distracts your attention from the present, just notice it. Without judging this or any other aspect of your experience, bring your attention back to the present moment and to your breath.

Formal mindfulness practices really help us increase self-awareness. They also have all sorts of benefits for us physiologically, such as strengthening certain areas of our brain that increase pleasant emotions and our sense of well-being. These types of exercises can also have benefits such as improving our immune system, reducing inflammation, and improving sleep.

And here's another informal mindfulness exercise you can do: google "mindfulness research" and read about all the other benefits of both formal and informal mindfulness practice. You'll be reading for a very long time!

Narrating or Witnessing

Although mindfulness might seem like a really simple thing to do, you'll probably find soon enough that putting it into practice isn't quite so easy. Some people find it more difficult than others; if you have additional challenges with concentrating such as those I mentioned earlier—ADD, ADHD, depression, anxiety—it will probably mean that mindfulness will be a little more challenging for you. When your emotions are more intense, mindfulness will definitely be harder to do. Sometimes you'll find, especially when you're still new at this, that you don't even think about the skill, never mind try to practice it.

All of this is normal. And to help you practice this skill, here's another tip, known as narrating, or witnessing. This is really about having a conversation with yourself about what your experience is, but doing so in a nonjudgmental, factual way—just as the narrator of a story or a witness at a trial is expected to do. In other words, you just talk to yourself about what you're doing: *I'm reading the words on the page. I notice that my attention is wandering to the schoolwork I have to do, and I'm feeling guilty that I'm reading this self-help book instead of doing my homework. I'm bringing my attention back to the book and trying to focus.* Or: *I'm focusing on my breath. I feel the air as it passes through my nostrils. I'm wondering if I should breathe out through my nostrils or my mouth. It's more comfortable for me to breathe through my nose, so that's what I'm doing. I notice I'm starting to worry that I'm not doing it right, but I'm going to do my best not to judge and just bring my attention back to my breath.*

You see in these examples that there are no judgments (for example, *I'm doing this wrong*); you're just observing your experience and then factually describing it to yourself. Again, this takes a lot of practice. One thing that can help is to label these thoughts and feelings as thoughts and feelings as they arise; for example, *I'm having the thought that I'm doing this wrong,* or *I'm feeling worried that I'm doing this wrong.* Explicitly naming the experiences in this way can help you be a little more objective about your experience instead of getting caught up in it.

Internal vs. External Experiences

You can practice mindfulness with internal or external experiences. Internal experiences are the events that take place within you—the thoughts you have, physical sensations, or emotions you feel. External experiences, obviously, are things that take place outside of you, which can be literally anything—the weather outside, the people around you, or the pictures on the wall.

This distinction is important, because some people are already really in tune with their internal experiences, and you can in fact be too in tune with these. The person with anxiety, for example, will be more likely to notice if his heart speeds up even just a bit; and this can become problematic because being overly focused on internal experiences can amplify them and make it hard to notice what's taking place around you. If this is you, you'll want to focus more on external experiences and take the attention off your internal events a bit.

But the opposite can also be true: some people are almost oblivious to their internal experiences and tend to really focus on external ones instead. It's important to have some awareness of what's going on inside of you, because this awareness is the first step in making changes. Remember what I said earlier about balance? This is a perfect example: you want to have a balance so that you're aware of both internal *and* external experiences, and not overly focused on either.

Developing Your Own Practice

Hopefully by now you're seeing how important mindfulness is, and all the ways that it can be helpful. If you're on board with this, though, you also need to recognize that mindfulness—like all the other skills you'll be reading about in this book—isn't just a technique you practice for a little while until things "get better" and then leave behind. Rather, mindfulness and the other DBT skills are about making life changes.

To that end, it's important to figure out ways to insert mindfulness into your life so you're practicing regularly. Ideally, you want to be doing both formal and informal practices. With formal practices, it can help if you choose a specific time of day that works best for you. For example, I'm an early riser and find that doing a formal practice in the afternoon inevitably means falling asleep, so I need to make time earlier in the day to practice. What time of day will work for you? Also, do you have a place to practice? While you don't have to have a silent place to practice, when you're first starting to do mindfulness it will be especially helpful if you have somewhere you won't be disturbed regularly. If you share a bedroom with your younger sibling, this might mean you go out into the backyard to do your practice or you start having an evening bath so you can do your breathing exercise in the tub.

As for informal practices, you'll do these wherever the task takes you. If you're driving mindfully (always a safe practice!), you'll obviously be doing this in the car; if you're practicing in math class, obviously you're doing this in the classroom. The biggest challenge with informal practices, often, is remembering to do them, so here are some high-tech tips:

* Put a reminder with an alarm in your smartphone, if you have one; book it as a recurring, daily appointment so your alarm goes off and you do your practice.

* You can download mindfulness bells on your computer, which will ring now and then to remind you to be mindful.

* There's an app for that! Check out all the mindfulness apps and find one that works for you.

And some low-tech tips:

* Put sticky notes on your dresser mirror, in the bathroom, or wherever else you'll see them first thing in the morning to remind you to practice.

* Choose one activity that you do every single day, at least once a day—like brushing your teeth, brushing

your hair, or eating breakfast—and make that your once-a-day practice. If you don't think about mindfulness at all throughout the day other than during that one activity, at least you've done it once. Of course, this is the minimum; ideally you'll remember to do it more often during the day.

You may be wondering: eyes open or closed? Mindfulness is best practiced with your eyes open, for a couple of reasons. First, for most people, the mind tends to wander more when the eyes are closed—we experience more memories and can see pictures more vividly, which causes our thoughts to wander. If you've had any traumatic experiences in your life and you experience intense memories, or if you have periods of time when you zone out or space out, you'll be more likely to have these experiences when your eyes are closed, so keep them open.

Also, the DBT philosophy with respect to mindfulness is that the goal is to live your life more mindfully, and it's difficult to go through life with your eyes closed. You want to be able to practice mindfulness whenever you want and wherever you are; if you get used to practicing mindfulness only with your eyes closed, the practice is less accessible to you.

Having said that, I also want to emphasize that it's important to be flexible. Some people find keeping their eyes open really difficult. If this is the case for you, you can close your eyes; just make it a goal to work toward keeping them open. Or you might find that you need to close your eyes for some formal practices—such as when you're trying to picture something in your head, which can be difficult to do with your eyes open—so you can close them then. Just remember that in general, it's going to be more effective for you to keep your eyes open.

Your Next Steps

In this chapter, I've introduced you to the core skill in DBT: mindfulness. I hope that you see how helpful this skill will be in reducing the painful emotions in your life, increasing the positive emotions in your life, and overall, helping you reach a more balanced state—in other words, how it will help you survive the emotional roller coaster!

You'll need to work hard to make sure you practice mindfulness regularly. At first, this might take a lot of energy and effort; just to remember to practice sometimes. But as you continue, like any skill it will start to come more naturally for you.

I'll incorporate mindfulness exercises throughout the book so you can learn a variety of ways to practice. If you're looking for more ways, google "mindfulness" and you'll find all sorts of resources; the technique or skill has become quite well known over the last couple of decades. For now, though, I'd like you to focus on two things: the breathing exercise you learned earlier in this chapter, and doing at least one thing every single day mindfully in an informal way. Remember, you want to be living your life more mindfully, so our goal right now is to get you thinking about it regularly. It doesn't matter how long you practice or what you do, but do at least one thing every single day mindfully. Gradually you'll likely notice mindfulness expanding to other areas in your life; you'll find that you're waking up.

In the next chapter, you'll be learning a lot of information you need to know about emotions so that you can work further on finding that balance in your life. The more you work on mindfulness now, the easier it will be to practice the other skills you'll be learning. So take your time, and don't rush through this book. Instead, focus on really learning and practicing the skills. If you notice you start to become impatient, as best as you can be gentle with yourself; this emotional roller coaster you're on is a way of being that you've probably known for most of your life—it's not something you can change in a day!

Chapter 2

What You Need to Know About Your Emotions

Hopefully you've been informally practicing mindfulness in your daily life as well as doing the formal breathing exercise you learned in the last chapter. Remember, this is the foundation for the other skills you're going to learn, so it's important that you're practicing and developing a good understanding of this and the other skills as we go along.

In this chapter, you're going to learn some important things about emotions. You'll also do some exercises to help you increase your awareness of your emotions and start to develop a different way of thinking about them. In doing so, you might learn that the way you've been relating to your emotions up until now has actually fed into the problems you have managing them.

What Is an Emotion?

We often refer to an emotion as a feeling, but this isn't quite accurate. While an emotion obviously involves how you feel, it's also much more than that.

In DBT, an emotion is thought of as a *full-system response*. In other words, an emotion involves how you feel (the feeling, such as anger, sadness, or happiness), as well as physical responses (changes in body chemistry and body language) and thoughts (including memories, images, and urges). For example, when you're feeling anxious, you don't just experience the feeling of anxiety. The fight-or-flight system in your body activates, pumping adrenaline into your system to help ready you either to stand and fight or to flee the situation; your body language, including your facial expression, changes (perhaps you look worried, anxious, or fearful); you experience anxious thoughts (*What if I can't do this?*), and you feel the urge to do something—with anxiety, this urge is often to run away to escape a situation, or to avoid it to begin with.

It's also important to realize that, while emotional responses are universal—people across the world experience the same emotions, and the emotional experiences are very similar (for example, we frown when we're angry)—no two emotional experiences are identical. While one person might get verbally aggressive when she's feeling angry, the next person might shut down and cry. In fact, this experience can also vary within the same person, depending on the situation she's in: when she's with her parents, she might become verbally aggressive and argue back, but when she's with her boyfriend, she might cry.

Some people don't actually know what they're feeling much of the time, and they walk around in an emotional "fog"; is this you? When you think about how you're feeling, does the word "bad" or "upset" often come to mind when there's a painful emotion of some sort? Do you try to ignore your emotions and avoid thinking about them altogether? This often contributes to the emotional roller coaster, in part because when people can't put a label or name on their emotions, they're less able to manage those emotions. So that's what's next: learning to name your emotions. If you think you're already able to do this, that's great—but I'd suggest you go through the exercises anyway, since doing so may teach you something, or at the very least confirm your belief in your awareness of and ability to accurately label your emotions.

Naming Your Emotions in Order to Manage Them

The first thing you need to do is stop using words like "bad" and "upset" to describe your emotional state. These words don't actually describe emotions and are too generic. What does "upset" mean? Angry? Anxious? Sad? It could mean any of these, so you need to be more specific about how you feel in order to figure out what to do about the emotion (if there is something that can be done). Let's do a mindfulness exercise to help you increase your awareness of emotions. You may want to read through this exercise first to familiarize yourself with it, and then practice it.

Exercise: Naming Your Emotions

Sitting quietly, bring your awareness to your body. Notice your posture, your body language, and your facial expression, and become aware of any physical sensations that might be present. Slowly expand your awareness from your body to any emotions that you feel in this moment, and as best as you can, observe them without judgment. Pay attention to what's happening in your body; just notice your thoughts, noting each experience to yourself without judgment, even if it's not what you would like it to be.

Next, gently bring your attention to your breath. Taking a deep breath and, slowly exhaling, ask yourself, *What emotion is here?* Allow your attention to be drawn to whatever emotion makes itself known. As best as you can, be open to it; observe it and describe it in as much detail as you can, sticking to the facts of your experience, and just noting the presence of the emotion. How does it feel in your body? If you can, name it. Whether you can label it or not, though, as best as you can, don't judge it; just acknowledge its presence.

When you do this exercise, you might find that you don't have any strong emotions; perhaps you feel simply content, curious, or even bored. Whatever's there, just notice it without judgment. If you're able to identify the emotion, repeat its name to yourself in an open and gentle way; for example, *satisfied, satisfied, satisfied* or *angry, angry, angry.* You might repeat the name of the emotion in time with your breath. If you find yourself getting caught up in the emotion or feeling overwhelmed by it, go back to focusing on your breathing until you feel less caught up.

Continue with this exercise for a few minutes (you might want to set a timer for two or three minutes so you don't have to keep thinking about the time), noticing any emotions that you become aware of and gently acknowledging them. If you can't find an emotion, that's fine; just acknowledge that. If you notice an emotion but can't name it, that's okay too. Just notice whatever your experience is of the emotion.

If you found you were unable to label your emotions with this exercise, don't worry—that's what this chapter is going to help you with. And if you were able to name your emotions, again that's great—but don't stop reading! Sometimes people are able to name some emotions and not others, and it's really important that you be very familiar with *all* your emotions.

Getting to Know Your Emotions

Next we'll look at six basic emotions in terms of the physical sensations and thoughts that often accompany them, as well as the situations in which they tend to arise. I suggest that you read through this list now and keep it handy so that you can refer to it when you have an emotional experience. In this way, over time, you'll better develop the skill of naming your emotions; or again you'll become confident that you're already able to do this. Keep an open mind, though—sometimes people are confident in these skills, but doing these exercises helps them realize that they actually tend to confuse one emotion for another. This confusion is especially common with anxiety and anger, so pay attention!

Anger

For some people, anger is almost a default emotion. If this is you, you'll notice that you become angry whenever anything emotional happens (for example, someone dies, and you feel anger rather than sadness; a friend tells you that you've hurt her feelings, and you feel angry rather than remorseful). So it's important to first think about when it's really appropriate or makes sense to feel anger. Here are some examples:

* When someone treats you disrespectfully (for example, insults you)

* When someone threatens you (emotionally or physically)

* When you're unable to reach an important goal

* When you believe that something is unfair or unjust; for example, that you have been treated unfairly, or that something happening in the world is unfair, perhaps after seeing a news report about animals being treated cruelly

Anger causes an adrenaline rush. It's part of the fight-or-flight response, in which your body gears up to either stand and fight (anger) or flee (fear). So when you experience anger, you'll often notice an increase in your heart rate and your breathing. Your breathing becomes shallow, you feel flushed, your muscles tense up, and you feel shaky. Your thoughts tend to become judgmental; for example, *What a jerk!* or *This shouldn't be happening; it's completely ridiculous.* As well, you might notice that your mind takes you back to other times when you've felt this angry. This is called *state-dependent memory,* when you are much better able to recall memories that continue to trigger the same emotion you're currently in (in other words, when you're depressed, you're able to remember other memories that feed into that depression; and when you're happy, you're better able to recall happy memories). Your mind is basically hunting for other times you've had this emotion, and the memories it comes up with increase the emotion you're currently feeling. Finally, the urges that often accompany anger are acting-out urges, such as the urge to yell or scream, to throw something or hit someone, or to lash out in verbally hurtful ways.

Here are some words to describe different types of anger:

Aggravated	Exasperated	Irritated
Annoyed	Frustrated	Mad
Bitter	Furious	Outraged
Bothered	Hostile	Resentful
Dissatisfied	Indignant	
Enraged	Irate	

Fear

Fear also causes an adrenaline rush and results in the same fight-or-flight response that anger does (although with fear, it's a little more complicated, since it can also result in a freezing response where you feel almost paralyzed). Your heart rate and breathing quicken, your breath becomes shallow, you feel flushed, your muscles tense up, you feel shaky, and so on. With fear, you might also find that you become dizzy or light-headed, feel nauseated, and experience discomfort in your chest.

Because the same fight-or-flight response is triggered when you feel anger or fear, the similar sensations can make it difficult to figure out which emotion you're feeling, so it's important to think hard about the situation you're in when the emotion arises, as well as your thoughts and urges in this situation.

Here are some examples of situations in which it would make sense to be afraid:

* When you're in a new or unfamiliar situation, or with people you don't know

* When someone or something is threatening you; for example, if someone picks a fight with you at a club or a dangerous-looking dog you don't know approaches you

* When someone you care about is being hurt or threatened

* When you think you may lose someone or something important to you; for example, if you fear during an argument with someone you care about that the relationship will end, or you fear that a disagreement with your teacher could lead to a poor mark in the class

Here are some words to describe different types of fear:

Afraid	Disconcerted	Disturbed
Alarmed	Distraught	Frantic
Anxious	Distressed	Nervous

Overwhelmed   Stressed   Worried

Panicked   Tense

Scared   Terrified

Sadness

How does sadness feel physically? The urge to cry often accompanies sadness, so you might experience tightness in your chest and throat. It's also common to feel tired or run-down, or to experience a decrease in your energy level, feel lethargic, or want to stay in bed all day. You might find that you don't get pleasure out of activities you once enjoyed, and that you feel empty inside. The urges that accompany sadness are often about isolating yourself and withdrawing from others.

Sadness arises for many different reasons. Here are some situations in which you would be likely to feel sad:

*   When you lose someone you care about; for example, through the end of a relationship or through death

*   When you're unable to meet an important goal (such as getting a job you wanted, or getting into the school you really wanted to go to, or being able to have a relationship with someone you had a crush on)

*   When someone you care about is feeling sad or hurt

Here are some words to describe different types of sadness:

Depressed	Forlorn	Miserable
Despairing	Glum	Sorrowful
Despondent	Grieving	Troubled
Disheartened	Heartbroken	Unhappy
Distressed	Hopeless	
Dreary	Low	

Shame or Guilt

First, let's look at the difference between shame and guilt. You feel guilt when you are acknowledging that you've done something wrong. Shame, on the other hand, arises when you feel that you are flawed as a person for whatever it is that you've done, that your actions negatively reflect who you are as a person. It makes sense, then, that you'll quite often experience both of these emotions at the same time—when you've done something that goes against your morals and values, you judge yourself for this, and you feel bad about yourself for what you've done. As with sadness, the urge with shame or guilt is often to hide away, to isolate yourself and withdraw from people around you. Here are some examples of when it would make sense to feel shame or guilt:

* When you do something that goes against your morals and values; for example, telling a lie or cheating on an exam

✱ When you are criticized in front of others

✱ When you think about, or are reminded of, something immoral you did in the past, or when someone else finds out that you did something immoral

✱ When someone whose opinion you value rejects or criticizes you for something you expected praise for; for example, when you do something you think is helpful for a group project and receive the feedback that you shouldn't have done it

Shame and guilt often come with some of the physical sensations that accompany sadness and fear. You might have the urge to cry and experience the tightness in your chest and throat that accompany this urge. People often blush and feel the nervousness that accompanies fear. You might also have an urge to try to rectify the situation; for example, if you've hurt someone, by trying to apologize or make up for the hurt you've inflicted.

Here are some words to describe different types of shame or guilt:

Apologetic	Embarrassed	Repentant
Ashamed	Guilty	Self-conscious
Blamed	Humiliated	Self-disgusted
Contrite	Mortified	Sorry
Degraded	Regretful	
Disgraced	Remorseful	

Love

Love is an emotion that you feel for other people, your pets, and hopefully yourself as well. You're likely to experience love in these kinds of situations:

* When you've developed feelings for someone because you're attracted to that person physically and emotionally

* When you see the pride in your parents' eyes when you've done something well, or when your parents tell you they love you

* When your dog greets you at the front door or cuddles up with you in bed; when your cat jumps into your lap, purring, or licks your face

When you experience the feeling of love, you likely experience an increase in positive emotions in general. You feel excited about seeing the person (or animal); you enjoy things more; you feel more secure, relaxed, and at peace. You might also notice an increase in your energy level and find you want to be with the person more often. Your thoughts will often be about the person—making plans for the future, thinking about the times you've spent together, and so on.

Here are some words to describe different types of love:

Accepted	Attraction	Connected
Adoring	Caring	Desiring
Affectionate	Cherishing	Devoted

Fondness   Longing   Passionate

Infatuated   Love-struck

Liking   Lust

Happiness

Happiness arises within you when things are going well. When you feel happy, you want to smile and to share your happiness with others. The urges that accompany happiness will depend on the situation you're happy about—you might want to hug someone you're happy to see; if you've received some news that has made you happy, you might feel excited and want to call people you care about to share that news. Happiness often makes people more active and social; you have more energy and want to do more things because you feel good.

But happiness is an emotion that we often have unrealistic expectations about. People often believe that they "should" feel happy, and they often question why they don't. In my experience, most of us don't live our lives in a state of happiness; we may feel content with life, or satisfied or peaceful, but I don't think the emotion of happiness is something that typically lasts a long time. When you do well on your SATs, get into the college you wanted, or get invited to prom, you'll feel happy; when you get that job you've been working toward, win an award at school, or reach some other big goal in your life, you'll feel happy. In other words, there will be events in your life that cause you to feel happy, but for the most part, that initial happiness will fade and turn into longer-lasting emotions like contentment, satisfaction, or peace.

Here are some words to describe different types of happiness:

Amused	Honored	Relieved
Content	Joyful	Satisfied
Delighted	Peaceful	Serene
Ecstatic	Pleased	Tranquil
Elated	Proud	
Glad	Relaxed	

Now that you have a better idea of how to name your emotions, or you've built your confidence that you already do this fairly accurately, you may want to return to the mindfulness exercise earlier in this chapter and practice naming your emotions some more before moving on.

The Role of Emotions

Next we're going to continue working on changing how you think about your emotions by looking at what function they serve. In other words, what's their role or job?

Yes, believe it or not, emotions serve an important purpose and we do need them—as uncomfortable as they can be at times, and as much as you might like to toss them out the window! In DBT, there are three reasons why we experience emotions.

Motivation

The first is that emotions motivate you, or prompt you to take action of some sort. Take bullying, for example. When students feel angered by bullying behaviors they see, they may feel motivated to take action and protest in some way; for example, by bringing these situations to the attention of principals and teachers, by participating in school campaigns to try to increase awareness and change the situation, or by creating awareness in other ways such as posting about it on Facebook. Without the anger that fuels these actions, the likelihood is that nothing would be done to try to change the situation.

Fear is also a motivating emotion. When your brain senses something that could be a threat to you, your fight-or-flight response primes you either to stand and fight or to run away from the situation. Either way, the emotion is motivating, prompting you to take some sort of action. Think about how useful this can be: You're walking home from school, and it's almost dark because you had to stay late for basketball practice. Suddenly you hear a noise behind you, and your fight-or-flight response kicks in. You become hyperalert; your senses are heightened as you try to figure out what the noise was and whether it's a danger to you. Your muscles tense; your heart rate increases. When you see two strangers walking toward you, you instinctively turn around and run back to a friend's house rather than risking your safety. The motivation triggered by your fear is what helped you get there safely.

Think about a time when you felt angry. What was the situation? Why did you feel that way? Can you think of what the anger was motivating you to do? And what about a time when you felt guilt? What was the function of the emotion in that situation?

Information

A second function of emotions is to provide you with information about a situation you want to change so that it's more suited to your wants or needs. Again, this could be the example of anger causing you to see that there is something about a situation that you believe is unfair, or that you don't like for another reason; or guilt and shame may arise to help you see that you're doing something that goes against your morals and values.

DBT tells us that your emotions may also communicate with you by providing you with emotional information before your brain has had time to rationally process and think about the information you're receiving from your senses. For example, you're out for a hike with your friends and you've taken the lead. Looking ahead, you see something coiled up in the middle of the path. Before your brain has time to process what you're seeing, fear kicks in to stop you and keep you safe from what could be a poisonous snake in the path.

Can you think of a time when your emotions provided you with information that helped you see you needed to act in a certain situation to try to make it different, more to your liking in some way? Or what about a time when your emotions provided you with information that caused you to act without having to take the time to think a situation through?

Communication

The last role of emotions is that of helping you communicate with others more effectively. The fact that emotions are associated with specific facial expressions and body language means that we're instinctively able to identify emotions in others, and they in us—which means that people around you will often be able to guess how you're feeling based solely on your facial expression and behavior. You don't have to tell someone that you're feeling sad when you're sobbing, or that you're feeling angry when you're clenching your fists and your jaw and your face is all red—they'll be able to guess pretty accurately what you're feeling. And when someone recognizes how you feel (or you recognize an emotion in someone else), that person can empathize with you; for example, attempting to console you with words or a hug when you're feeling sad, or trying to help you calm down when you're angry.

Your emotions might also motivate you to verbally communicate with others about something—such as the earlier example of anger, which might motivate you to try to change a situation you're not happy with.

Can you think of a time when your emotions served this function for you? Maybe a time when you were feeling down and, recognizing this, a friend tried to cheer you up? Or can you think of a time when you noticed someone was feeling an emotion that motivated you to act in a certain way toward her?

It's important to recognize that, although your emotions are there to serve a purpose, they aren't foolproof, and you can't take them as facts. Just because you feel something doesn't make it true; you have to evaluate it. Just because something smells good doesn't mean it tastes good, so when you're trying a food for the first time, you're often cautious about it, testing to see if your sense of smell is correct. Likewise, consider an optical illusion: your vision tells you that you see one thing, but you question this, recognizing that your vision is fallible and might be playing tricks on you.

Your emotions are the same; they're another sense, providing you with more information, but they could also be leading you astray. So just because you feel threatened by the strangers walking behind you doesn't necessarily mean they plan to assault you. Just because you're frightened by the coil in the middle of the path doesn't mean it's a danger to your well-being. We'll look at this further in a bit, but it's an important thing to remember: your emotions have a job, yes—but they don't always do it perfectly!

Now we're going to look at another way that your emotions can often be confusing, which is in relation to the thoughts and behaviors associated with them.

The Connection Between Emotions, Thoughts, and Behaviors

Remember when we talked about an emotion as being a full-system response? This is one of the reasons emotions can be so confusing—there's a lot going on all at the same time. So you're *feeling* an emotion while you're *thinking* certain thoughts triggered by that emotion and engaging in *behaviors* related to that emotion. Because of this, people often confuse the emotion itself with thoughts and behaviors. Take a look at the following diagram:

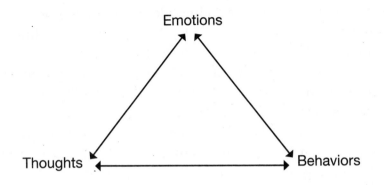

The arrows demonstrate that changing your emotions will change your thoughts and behaviors; changing your thoughts will change your emotions and behaviors; and changing your behaviors will change your emotions and thoughts. Because these three areas are so interrelated, it's really easy to confuse them. Often when I ask someone how she feels about something, I'll get a description of thoughts instead. For example, if I asked how you felt when you realized there were strangers following you, you might respond "I wanted to get out of there," or "I wanted to run as fast as I could," which are thoughts; the emotion associated with these thoughts would be something like "scared" or "anxious."

One reason that this confusion occurs is because this full-system response happens so quickly and automatically that you don't usually stop to process what's going on before you act. But if you think about it, acting without stopping to think is probably one of the main reasons your emotions get you into trouble, so it's really important that you learn to separate your emotions from your thoughts and behaviors. The naming emotions exercise you did earlier will help with this, but now your job is to figure out what you're feeling (don't forget to refer back to the list of emotions if you need to) versus what you're thinking (your thoughts about the situation, including images, memories, and urges) and how you're behaving (not what you felt like doing or wanted to do, but the actions you actually took). Let's go back to our previous example and break this down further.

You're walking home from school by yourself, it's getting dark, and you hear a noise. Your experience would probably go something like this: *Oh my gosh, what was that?* (thought). You look around, trying to assess the situation (behavior), and you see people you don't know behind you. *Someone's following me. What if they attack me?* (thought). You feel afraid (emotion). *There are three of them. I'll never be able to fight them off. There's no one around to help me* (thought). Your fear increases (emotion). You have an urge to run and escape the situation (thought); you consider what you should do (thought). You turn around and run back the way you came, to your friend's house (behavior).

Let's look now at how you might change the outcome of this situation if you change one aspect of your experience.

You're walking home from school by yourself, it's getting dark, and you hear a noise. Your initial thought is *Oh my gosh, what was that?* (thought). You look around, trying to assess the situation (behavior), and you see people you don't know behind you. You think, *I wonder who they are. They don't look familiar* (thought). You feel curious (emotion). You continue to observe them (behavior), noting that they are three teenaged girls (thought). *I see them looking at a map and looking at the street sign; it looks as though they're lost* (thought). You consider what you should do (thought). Because it's getting dark out, you feel some concern for them (emotion). You approach and ask if they need help finding their way (behavior).

So here are two very different outcomes based on the same beginning scenario. Do you see how your emotions and behaviors can be influenced by changing your thoughts about the situation? Let's look at one more example to help you understand this.

You come home from school and tell your parents that you got a C on your chemistry test (behavior). You're already feeling disappointed in yourself for this (emotion) and you're worried (emotion) that this could affect whether you get accepted to the college you want (thought). When your parents express the same concern, you feel angry with them (emotion); you think, *They're always disappointed in me!* (thought) and you yell at them and storm off to your room (behavior).

Again, let's look at an alternate outcome that might result from changing something about this experience.

You come home from school and tell your parents that you got a C on your chemistry test (behavior). You're already feeling disappointed in yourself for this (emotion) and you're worried (emotion) that this could affect whether you get accepted to the college you want (thought). When your parents express the same concern, you feel angry with them (emotion); you think, *They're always disappointed in me!* (thought). You notice this thought and talk back to it: *They're disappointed* for *me because they see that I'm disappointed in myself* (thought). You express your worry to them (behavior) and they provide some reassurance, which further helps you change your thinking and your emotions about your chem grade.

Before you say "Easier said than done!" remember that these are just examples I'm giving you to demonstrate the idea right now. Of course, it takes a lot of practice for you to be able to change your thoughts, emotions, or behaviors; first you have to understand why and how it will be helpful, and then you have to start putting into practice the little steps I've given you so far: namely, practicing mindfulness to help you become more aware of these experiences so that over time you'll be able to change them. To help with this, though, there's one more thing you need to know about, and that's the role of your interpretations in all of this.

The Role of Interpretations

You've probably started to see in the previous examples how your thinking gets in the way a lot! You're constantly interpreting your experiences, so that you can have two very different outcomes from the same situation. What's important to recognize here is that you're very rarely reacting to a situation itself (though this does happen sometimes, as when you reacted to the thing coiled in the path and your brain went into fight-or-flight mode, causing you to act). More often, you're reacting to your *interpretation* of the situation. The following diagram demonstrates this idea:

Situation ⟶ Interpretation ⟶ Emotion

So if we apply this to the previous example of the chemistry test, this is what we get:

Parents' reaction ⟶ Thought that they're disappointed in you ⟶ You feel hurt

The good news is that practicing the skills you're learning in this book will help you step back from these automatic thoughts and interpretations, recognize them as such, and think about how you'd like to act rather than just reacting.

Thoughts and Emotions Are Not Facts

If you continue along this line of thinking, you'll also see that the thoughts and emotions you experience aren't facts. I alluded to this earlier when we looked at your emotions as being just another sense: just because you *feel* a certain way doesn't mean that it's a reflection of reality. For example, just because you felt your parents were disappointed in you doesn't mean it was true. In this instance, you were feeling disappointed in yourself, and therefore you interpreted their reaction as disappointment in you as well.

When you can remember that your emotions are usually a response to your interpretation of events, you can often see more clearly that while your emotions makes sense, it might not be warranted if your thoughts about the situation aren't accurate. Remember, if your emotions are just another sense, you need to factor this into the rest of your experience and assess. And believe it or not, you're not always right! Similarly, when you have thoughts about a situation, they're not necessarily an accurate reflection of reality—you can (and should) factor them in, but once again you need to assess.

One way of helping you see that your thoughts and emotions aren't facts (or anything you have to remain attached to) is to practice being mindful to these experiences: just watching or observing them. The following mindfulness exercises will help you do just that. You'll probably want to read through these exercises first; then choose one, set a timer for just a couple of minutes to start, and practice.

Exercise: Observing Your Thoughts and Emotions in a Stream

Sitting in a comfortable position, close your eyes and imagine yourself standing in a shallow stream. The water comes to just above your knees, and a gentle current pushes against your legs. As you stand in the stream, notice as thoughts and emotions slowly start to float by. Don't try to hold on to them as they glide past you, and as best as you can, don't get caught up in them; just notice them as they float past you. When you notice yourself getting caught up thinking about a thought or an emotion, come back to just watching. Return your attention to just observing your thoughts and emotions. As best you can, don't judge the thoughts or feelings that float by; just become aware of their presence.

Exercise: Observing Your Thoughts and Emotions in Clouds

Imagine yourself lying in a field of grass, looking up at the fluffy white clouds. In each cloud you see a thought or a feeling; just observe each thought or feeling as it slowly floats by. As best as you can, don't judge them, try to push them away, or hold on to them. Just observe them as they float through the sky. Don't try to grab the thoughts or emotions, and don't get caught up thinking about them—just notice them. When you realize you've gotten carried away with a particular cloud, bring yourself back to lying in the field of grass. When you notice your attention has wandered from the exercise, bring your attention back to observing and labeling the thoughts and emotions, without judging yourself.

Your Next Steps

One of our goals here is to change the relationship you've had with your emotions. Up until now, they've probably been a big source of trouble for you: when you're on the emotional roller coaster, the ups and downs can be scary and painful, and can have a lot of negative consequences. But think of your emotions as just one more sense. Just like your sight, hearing, taste, touch, and smell, your emotions are there to provide you with another piece of the puzzle to help you learn and make decisions. Do you hate your sense of smell? Probably not. What about your vision? Life would be difficult without it. So as best as you can, don't judge your emotions (you'll learn a skill that will help with this in chapter 5), and practice thinking of them as just another sense, providing you with information.

Next we'll be looking at more concrete skills so you can put all the information you've learned about emotions in this chapter to use. For now, you really need to practice, practice, practice—noticing your emotions and naming them; noticing your thoughts; telling the difference between emotions, thoughts, and behaviors; and remembering that your emotions and thoughts are not facts. Remember, these are the building blocks; the practice you do now will ensure you have a strong foundation to build on as you work your way through this book.

Chapter 3

Slowing Down the Emotional Roller Coaster

Being on the emotional roller coaster, or having problems regulating your emotions, means that you react to things that others typically wouldn't react to, your reaction is more intense than what others consider to be warranted in the situation, and it takes you longer to return to your usual self. If you recall from the introduction of this book, this emotion dysregulation is caused in part by your biology, but that doesn't mean there's nothing you can do about it.

In this chapter, you'll learn about three different ways we have of thinking about things, you'll learn some techniques to help you slow the roller coaster down so you have a little more control, and you'll learn about some lifestyle choices you may be making that contribute to the roller coaster you're currently on.

Three Ways of Thinking

DBT teaches that we all have three different ways of thinking about things, or different states of mind: our reasoning self, our emotional self, and our wise self. People who are riding the emotional roller coaster, of course, tend to think about things more often from their emotional selves, but there are two other thinking perspectives, and it's important that you practice accessing these different states in order to improve your ability to manage your emotions. In this section we'll look at each way of thinking so you can practice getting to know your own states of mind.

Emotional Self

Let's start with the one you probably know best—your emotional self. When you're thinking and acting from your emotional self, your behaviors are being controlled by your emotions. So if you're feeling angry, you lash out even if your anger has nothing to do with the person you're lashing out at. Or if you're feeling anxious, you avoid the thing that's causing the anxiety; for example, you skip class so you don't have to do the presentation you were scheduled to do today, or you decide to stay home instead of going to the social event you were supposed to attend with your family.

When you're acting from your emotional self, you are *reacting* from your emotions, instead of *choosing how to act*. It feels as though your emotions are in control, and you're just along for the ride. When you're in this state, you often do things that you regret later on, like lashing out at someone you care about, or acting impulsively in ways that have negative consequences in the long run (like getting drunk at your uncle's wedding, skipping class when you really need to get a good grade, or breaking up with your girlfriend because you're angry with her). If you've been on the emotional roller coaster, this probably sounds all too familiar. But the good news is, there are other ways of thinking about things, and you can change your thinking style with some work.

Reasoning Self

When you're in your reasoning self, you're using your straightforward, logical thinking, considering only the facts of the situation. There are usually no emotions in this state; if there are emotions, they're minimal and not affecting how you behave. Some examples of reasoning-self behavior would include choosing a college based only on the programs offered, the likelihood of getting a job after graduating, and the school's reputation, rather than considering things such as how convenient you want visiting home to be, whether you have any friends attending that college, and whether you like the look and feel of the campus. Daily examples of when you might be in your reasoning self would be things like doing your homework (if you're focused on doing your homework, and not feeling so frustrated with math that you throw your book out the window!) or following the directions your parents left you to get dinner started on a night they'll both be home late.

While most people on the emotional roller coaster will be more familiar with the emotional self, sometimes people are on that roller coaster because they regularly disregard their emotions and values and act mostly from their logic or reasoning, which can also have negative consequences. In other words, if you tend to ignore what your emotions and values are telling you, you're probably not acting in your best interest very often, and this will often trigger emotional pain such as anger, disappointment, and frustration. With this skill, what we want to focus on is finding a balance between listening only to your emotions and listening only to your reasoning; this is where your wise self comes in.

Wise Self

Your wise self is the balance between your emotional self and your reasoning self. Instead of choosing one or the other, your wise self has you consider both of these elements—your emotions *and* your reasoning—and also factors in a third component, which is your gut instinct, or intuition. You allow yourself to feel your feelings, and you consider what your reasoning or logic is saying, but you also listen to that little voice inside of you that has weighed the possible consequences (positive and negative) and is telling you what's most effective in the long run.

Can you identify a time when your wise self was trying to get your attention? You might not always listen to it, but it's there. And it's important to remember that what your inner wisdom tells you to do isn't always the thing that's easy to do, or even what you want to do; rather, it's what's going to be best for you, for the situation, and for others when all is said and done.

Let's look at an example to make these three ways of thinking more clear.

✳ Michelle's Story

Michelle is in eleventh grade and is considering what colleges she'll apply to next year. Her emotional self is telling her she should apply to College A, because that's where Karsten, her boyfriend, plans to go, and she really wants to keep their two-year relationship going. She can't stand the thought of being at school without him, and she's also feeling anxious that, if they were to go to different schools, he would meet someone else and they'd break up.

Michelle's reasoning self, on the other hand, is telling her she should apply to College B, because they have a top-notch journalism program, and it's been her dream to become an investigative reporter. College B also has a school newspaper with a really great reputation, and many of the editors from that paper have gone on to work at some of the biggest newspapers in the country.

But what about Michelle's wise self? She wants to stay in a relationship with Karsten and fears that this won't be possible if they go to separate schools, so she should go to College A, but she can see the benefits of attending College B for her career aspirations. Her inner wisdom, that little voice inside, tells her she needs to think about her future. While she'd like to stay with Karsten, there's no guarantee the relationship will work out even if they do go to the same school; they're still quite young and might head in different directions in their lives. And if they can't handle being apart for long periods for a few years while they're in school, how would they stay together when she's off traveling for weeks at a time as a reporter? Also, Karsten has made it very clear that he's putting his career goal of being a lawyer before their relationship, so her inner wisdom is telling her she shouldn't be the one making all the sacrifices—that's not the kind of relationship she wants, and she knows, deep down, that she'd end up resenting Karsten for it.

So you can see here that Michelle's wise self isn't telling her to do what's easy, or even necessarily what she wants to do; instead, it's helping her see what's in her best interest and the best interest of the relationship in the long run. She's allowing herself to feel her emotions while she thinks logically about the facts of the situation, and at the same time she's bringing her intuition into play to help her make this difficult decision.

Finding Balance

This is another area that's about finding balance in your life: you don't want to *only* be in your emotional self, and you don't want to *only* be in your reasoning self. Both of these states of mind are helpful and necessary at times; for example, your emotional self also encompasses enjoyable emotions such as love, joy, and excitement, so you don't want to miss out on those intense emotions, and of course you need your reasoning self to help you think logically about situations. But the goal here is to be able to access your wisdom more often—to balance your emotions with your reasoning, and bring in your intuition to help you make wiser, healthier choices.

It's important to recognize that this is something we do on a daily basis; it's not just something that comes into play when we have big, life-altering decisions to make. It could be the decision you make to get out of bed at 7:15 a.m. instead of 7:30 a.m. so you have time for breakfast, or to not badger your younger brother when he's hogging the TV remote. There are often small times in your daily life when you're acting from your wise self; you just don't always see it. And it's important that you start to see it so you can give yourself credit for those times. Of course, it's also important that you be aware of when you're acting from your emotional or reasoning self, because when you're in these states you want to have the option of moving toward your wise self.

How to Get to Your Wise Self

Like any new skill, accessing your inner wisdom will take a lot of practice and energy at first, but I hope you won't let that discourage you. These skills are all worth the effort you put in, because they are skills that will help bring a new peace and calmness to your life, helping you survive that emotional roller coaster. And as you continue to practice, these skills will start to come more naturally. For now, though, let's take a look at some of the ways you can work on getting to your wise self.

Increasing Self-Awareness

When you're trying to make any kind of change, the first thing you need to work on is increasing your awareness of yourself. So with these skills, you need to practice being aware of what thinking style you're in on a regular basis. Once you develop this awareness, you'll be able to choose whether you want to do something about it—in other words, if you notice you're on the emotional roller coaster, you'll have the option of using skills to help you access your wise self. So how do you develop this self-awareness? Observe. Notice. Acknowledge. You don't have to write anything down about what you observe and notice, although some people find this helps them pay more attention; the idea is to bring your awareness to your experience as often as possible. Ask yourself multiple times throughout the day, *What thinking style am I using right now?* Or *Am I listening to my wise self?* Or *What is my wise self telling me to do in this situation?* And just notice whatever is going on in you at that moment, without judging it; in other words, be mindful of your experience.

Narrating or Witnessing Your Experience

In chapter 1, we looked at the mindfulness skill of narrating, or witnessing, when you talk to yourself about what you're doing to help you stay in the present moment. This can be a helpful skill when it comes to noticing what state of mind you're in as well.

To go back to Michelle's example, it might go something like this: *I'm thinking about the future and worrying about my relationship with Karsten if we don't go to the same school. My throat feels tight and I want to cry as I picture him meeting someone new and we break up. I'm feeling sad and anxious—I'm in my emotional self right now.* Or *I'm thinking of all the logical, factual reasons I should go to College B. I'm not feeling any emotions or allowing my values to influence me as I'm considering my options. I'm in my reasoning self right now.* Or finally, *I'm feeling a bit anxious as I'm thinking about this decision I have to make. I'm considering how I'll feel about each college as well as thinking about the positive and negative consequences of each option. Even though I'm feeling anxious, I'm not letting my anxiety make the decision for me. I'm in my wise self right now.*

Breathing Well

This might sound funny, but believe it or not, most of us don't breathe properly—especially when emotions start to intensify and the emotional self starts to take over. So changing your breathing can actually help you access your wise self.

Pay attention to your breath for a moment, and notice where you're breathing from right now: Is it your chest? Your abdomen? Or maybe somewhere in between? People who are anxious on a regular basis tend to breathe shallowly, from the chest. But even if you're breathing well right now, in this moment, chances are that when emotions start to intensify, your breathing becomes shallower—this is just something that happens in that full-system emotional response we looked at in the last chapter.

Breathing deeply from your abdomen sends signals to your brain that you are relaxed, so that, even if you don't feel relaxed, it will gradually help you get there. What this means when you're feeling intense emotions isn't that you're going to feel totally calm and at peace, but that your emotions will come down a notch or two and at least become a little more bearable. Deep breathing also sends more oxygen to the thinking parts of your brain, which will help you access your inner wisdom, so you can think about what to do that might further help reduce the painful emotions you're experiencing.

Most of us forget how to breathe properly at some point in our lives, probably in part because as we get older our stress levels tend to increase, and we tend to hold tension and stress in our abdominal muscles; when our abdominal muscles are tight, it makes it harder to breathe deeply. So in this exercise, we're going to review how to breathe properly, using your diaphragm.

Exercise: Abdominal Breathing

First, take a moment to notice your breath. Is it deep or shallow? What's moving more when you inhale, your chest or your belly (or perhaps somewhere in between)? Notice the pace of your breath: are you breathing quickly or slowly? (Here's a tip: you should be taking approximately ten to twelve inhalations per minute.)

Now lean back comfortably in a chair (but don't get so comfortable that you might fall asleep—remember, mindfulness is about waking up to your life). Place your fingers on your stomach so that their tips are just slightly touching, right around your belly button. When you breathe in, you want to see your fingertips rise slightly as your belly inflates; as you exhale, your fingertips will come back together again as your stomach deflates. Think of your stomach as a balloon: when you put air in, it inflates; when you let the air out, it deflates.

Breathing this way may feel forced or unnatural for you right now, and that's okay—do it anyway! If you get dizzy or light-headed, you're breathing too fast, so as best as you can, slow it down. You may find you have to push the air down into your diaphragm to inflate your belly; if you find this really hard, you can try doing this exercise lying down, which makes it a little easier to get the air down further, past your chest. Do this for a few moments, being mindful of your breath, just noticing how it feels to breathe deeply. Watch your belly as it rises and falls with each breath, and when you notice your attention has wandered, bring it back to the present, as best as you can without judging.

This is called abdominal, or diaphragmatic, breathing—breathing from your diaphragm, which is the muscle that sits underneath your lungs and helps them breathe. This is how you are supposed to breathe, and it's how you breathe when you're fast asleep or completely relaxed. Remember, breathing this way is breathing as though you're relaxed, which sends signals to your brain that you *are* relaxed, which in fact helps you relax!

Again, breathing this way can help you calm yourself when you're experiencing intense emotions. But don't fall into the trap of using this (or any other) mindfulness exercise only when you "need" it. If you consciously breathe this way on a regular basis, your body will naturally start to breathe this way on its own. That means that your overall level of painful emotions will decrease. Of course, don't forget that the more you practice something, the more it comes naturally to you, so once you've been practicing this for a while, you'll also have an easier time using this exercise to help yourself feel calmer when your emotions are heightened.

Your Physical Health Can Affect Your Thinking Style

Over the last couple of decades, we've developed a better under-standing of the connection between the body and the mind, and we've been recognizing that the way we treat our bodies really affects our minds, and vice versa. In this section, we're going to look at the DBT skills that reduce your vulnerability to your emotional self. In other words, we'll look at some choices you might be making in your life that are actually making you more vulnerable to being controlled by your emotions, and how making changes in some of these areas might improve your ability to get off—or at least slow down—the emotional roller coaster.

Balancing Sleep

You've probably noticed that when you don't get enough sleep you're more irritable, grumpy, and lethargic. Your energy level is lower than usual, it's probably harder for you to get motivated to do things, and your concentration and memory aren't what they normally are. You may or may not have noticed that many of these same things happen when you *over*sleep. Remember: balance. In order to reduce the likelihood of your emotional self taking over, you need to get enough sleep, but not too much. The following tips can help improve your sleep.

Get Comfortable

First and foremost, make sure that you're as comfortable as possible when you sleep:

* If you can, adjust the temperature in your room to suit you.

* If possible, make sure your bed is comfortable.

* Make your bedroom as dark as possible when it's time for bed. Ambient light from electronic devices

actually sends signals to your brain that it's daytime, so make sure to turn off your computer and other electronics.

* Turn off the television! Your brain continues to process sensory input from the environment even when you're sleeping, so even though you're not aware of it, you're still listening to the TV.

  Quick story: I had a client once who didn't really buy this; she slept with the TV on all the time. One day she came to session and said that she had begun sleeping with the TV off, then explained how this happened. One night she was asleep and woke suddenly to screams. She was convinced that her sister was being attacked in the next room until she realized it was a television show. This client slept with the TV on because she said she needed the noise; now instead of the TV, she listens to nature CDs that don't stimulate her brain.

* Find a new place for your pets to sleep. This is a tough one for me to say because I'm an animal lover, but the fact is that when you have pets sleeping in your bed with you, you don't sleep as well. It's true. The research tells us this. (And yet my two small dogs sleep with me every night!) If you have problems with insomnia, you really do need to find somewhere else for your pets to sleep.

If you've tried these tips and sleep is still difficult for you, or you find that you sleep okay but you're tired all the time, talk to your doctor. Of course, stress and other emotional difficulties can interfere with sleep, but there are also medical problems that can contribute to these issues. And we all know how it feels and what it does to the rest of your life when you're not sleeping properly, so if there's anything that can be done to improve your sleep, it's worth trying.

Reduce Caffeine and Other Stimulants

Most people know that caffeine is a stimulant and can keep you awake at night. Coffee (and related drinks like espresso or cappuccino), tea, chocolate, energy drinks like Red Bull, and obviously caffeine pills and other medications that contain caffeine (check with your pharmacist if you're not sure) are therefore stimulants and will negatively affect your sleep. And caffeine stays in your system for about fourteen hours, so even if you're drinking your last coffee at noon, it could still be affecting how you sleep at night.

Because we're all different, and because many people are so attached to their caffeine, I suggest that you do a two-week experiment: Cut caffeine out of your diet. You may have to do this slowly because you'll go through withdrawal (usually appearing as headaches and irritability); I recommend staying caffeine-free for two weeks because it will take time for you to withdraw from the caffeine. Then pay attention to what you're like without it. How is your sleep? Your irritability? Your anxiety? Be honest with yourself and really notice if there are any differences. There may not be. If you don't notice any differences, you can slowly reintroduce caffeine into your life, again paying attention as you do so to any changes in these areas. But if you do notice changes, you have a decision to make: is it worth going back to your caffeine product of choice?

Here's another quick story: my client Teresa decided to do the two-week experiment. When I first met her, she was drinking six extra-large coffees every day. She didn't manage to stop drinking caffeine altogether, but she did get down to one extra-large coffee every day, and she reported that not only was she sleeping better and feeling less anxious, but her relationships had actually improved because she was less irritable!

The thing is, when you're already on the emotional roller coaster, substances such as caffeine usually only add to the emotional ups and downs—if stopping, or even reducing, can help you manage your emotions more effectively, isn't it worth a try?

Balancing Eating

There's that word again: balance. You may have noticed that when you don't eat enough, you experience physical sensations such as shakiness or trembling, light-headedness or dizziness, headaches, and rapid heartbeat; many people experience irritability and mood swings as well. Studies have shown that not eating enough feeds into symptoms of depression and anxiety.

Overeating, on the other hand, also increases the likelihood of emotions taking over, as you might get judgmental of yourself and feel guilty for overindulging.

I like to use the car analogy. If you don't keep putting fuel in the car, and the right kind of fuel (that is, regular versus diesel; or nutritious foods versus empty calories), you're going to run out of gas. Our bodies need calories just to breathe, digest, blink, and stand upright. If you're not regularly putting fuel into your body, it's going to have to use the fuel that would go to other tasks such as concentrating, remembering things, or going for a walk to do the imperative tasks that keep you alive and functioning properly. So when you don't eat well, your body suffers, and part of this suffering is a toll on your emotional and mental health. The key, then, is to make sure you're eating enough and not regularly overeating.

Reducing (or Eliminating) Use of Drugs and Alcohol

Drugs and alcohol are called mood-altering substances for an obvious reason—they alter your mood—and you have no control over how your mood is altered. Some people find that sometimes alcohol helps them relax, so they feel calmer and less anxious in social situations, for example, which helps them enjoy themselves more. But alcohol lowers your inhibitions, causing you to do things you wouldn't normally do when you haven't been drinking—and this often means acting from your emotional self, and behaving in ways you later regret.

I've worked with many clients who have problems with anger and become explosive when they've been drinking. Mick, for example, broke more than one cell phone when he'd been drinking by throwing it when he got angry, and he lost his relationship with his girlfriend because he would become so verbally aggressive that she wasn't comfortable being around him when he was drinking.

Drugs other than alcohol often have these same effects, as well as others that can put you and your emotional health at risk; for example, cocaine and other stimulants can create anxiety and even cause symptoms of psychosis—being out of touch with reality, such as seeing or hearing things that aren't actually there, which will obviously put you at risk for being controlled by your emotions. Marijuana, although many people believe it to be harmless, can also trigger your emotional self, whether it's the lack of motivation that often comes with regular use of marijuana, or the anxiety and depression that some people experience.

Substance use also comes with aftereffects quite often: with alcohol you have the hangover the next day, and with many drugs you have the "crash" after the high. When I was working with Mick, he realized, over time, that his use of alcohol and marijuana would actually leave him feeling depressed and anxious, with an increase in mood swings, for about three days.

So now is a good time to begin assessing this for yourself: if you use drugs or alcohol, start noticing, *honestly* noticing, how these substances affect you—not just when you're using, but in the days afterward as well.

Increasing Exercise

Of course we all know—and we hear regularly—about how important it is to get enough exercise, but did you know that some studies have found that cardiovascular exercise (exercise that increases your heart rate) can actually be as effective at reducing symptoms of depression as an antidepressant medication? It's true. When you get your heart rate going during exercise, your brain releases "feel-good" chemicals called endorphins that increase your sense of well-being. So not only is exercise good for your body, it's great for your mind.

It's not always easy to find time to exercise, especially in today's world where you're under pressure to do well in school so you can get into a good college so you can have a fabulous career! And there's pressure to work hard to earn money so you can have the latest gadgets. You have chores to do, clubs you want to belong to, volunteer work you should do... The list goes on and on. So how do you make time? Walking fast can get your heart rate up, so take a walk at school. Ride your bike to school when the weather's nice instead of taking the bus, or sign up to play a sport at school or in a community league. And if you have access to a swimming pool, you're set for warm weather—do some laps. Get creative. You don't necessarily have to find time to go to a gym, but you can do that too if it's something you enjoy. Teaming up with a partner is often more motivating, so ask your best friend to start walking home from school with you now and then. You could even double the value and start earning some money after school by becoming the neighborhood dog-walker!

My guideline for exercise is that you're going to benefit from anything more than what you're doing now. So introduce exercise into your life in some way, and it will do you good physically and emotionally, as well as reduce the likelihood that you will be controlled by your emotions. And who knows? You might even like it!

Taking Care of Yourself Physically

While taking care of yourself physically includes exercise and eating properly and all the other things we've talked about in this section, what I'm talking about here is treating physical health conditions you may have. Many people have conditions such as diabetes, asthma, migraines, or chronically painful conditions, which make them more likely to be controlled by their emotional selves. To reduce the influence of these conditions on your emotions, you have to do your best to manage them. In other words, check your blood sugar regularly and take your insulin; take your asthma medication the way you're supposed to; avoid the foods and other triggers for your migraines; and take your medications as prescribed and attend your physiotherapy or other treatments required for your physical pain conditions.

The same also holds true for acute illnesses you may develop. When you get a cold, a stomach bug, or strep throat, you've probably noticed you're more irritable and grumpy. You want others to comfort you, and you're quicker to snap when things don't go your way. In other words, you're more emotional than usual. When this is going on, you need to take good care of yourself: get your rest, get proper nutrition as best as you can, ask others for help if you have responsibilities you need to take care of, and so on. If you're prescribed medications or you could benefit from some over-the-counter remedies, make sure you take them. And most of all, practice self-awareness: you're more likely to be controlled by your emotional self when you're sick, so being aware of this can help prevent you from getting on that emotional roller coaster!

Your Next Steps

In this chapter, you've learned about the three thinking styles we all have, and you've learned about the mind-body connection with respect to the lifestyle choices you may be making that can feed into your emotions. The more you ignore your body, the more likely you are to be overtaken by your emotions. On the other hand, when you're taking good care of yourself—by balancing sleep and eating, reducing (or eliminating) use of drugs and alcohol, increasing exercise, and taking care of chronic and acute physical illnesses—you're increasing your chances of surviving the roller coaster and getting to your wise self.

So for your next steps, the first thing you need to do is start to increase your awareness of what state of mind you're in: just ask yourself now and then, *What state of mind am I in?* Or *Am I using my wise self right now?* The more you get into the routine of paying attention, the more quickly you'll notice when you're not acting from your wisdom, and that of course means that you'll have choices about what to do about it.

The second thing is to do a bit of a self-assessment: of the five areas we've just looked at that increase your emotional self, which one do you most need to work on? The key here is to be honest with yourself. This isn't about judgment; it's about acknowledging what is so that you can decide if you're willing to start making changes. So really think about each of these areas, and ask yourself, *Is this something I need to work on?* When you find an area you answer yes to, the next step is to set a small, realistic, achievable goal for yourself. So if you decide you need to work on reducing your drinking, setting a goal of eliminating drinking altogether might not be realistic (it may be; it really depends on you, so you'll have to decide this for yourself). But you might instead decide that you're going to have only two drinks when you're out with friends from now on, instead of not worrying about how much you have to drink. Or you might decide that you can drink, but only once a month. You might also decide, by the way, that you can't do this alone and you need some help—if you have even the slightest feeling this is the case, I hope you can stick to that honesty and ask someone for help, whether it's a parent, a teacher, or someone at a crisis line. You don't have to do it alone.

Here's another example: Let's say you decide that you need to work on eating better. If you're currently eating only dinner, it's not going to be realistic and it likely won't be achievable for you to go from eating one meal a day to eating three meals and two snacks. So ask yourself, *Of breakfast and lunch, which will be easier for me to commit to working on?* You might decide that, since you never feel hungry in the morning, lunch will be easier to start with, so this becomes your goal: to eat lunch four out of seven days this week. It doesn't have to be a big lunch; as with exercise, my belief is that anything more than what you're doing now is going to benefit you. So start off small. Bring a yogurt for lunch, or a piece of fruit, cheese and crackers, or a granola bar. Once you've gotten used to this, you can increase your goal to eating lunch daily, and then to eating a larger lunch. Next you can work on eating something small for breakfast, and so on.

The idea, though, is to set small, realistic goals. If you set your goals too high, what often happens is that you don't reach your goal, you beat yourself up, you throw the goal out the window, and nothing changes. So take baby steps; have patience and things will slowly change. And over time, with these concrete lifestyle changes, you will likely find that your emotional roller coaster will begin to slow down.

In the next chapter, we'll look at some DBT skills that will help you start to reduce the intensity of your painful emotions, which will make those emotions more tolerable. But remember, baby steps—rushing through this book will get you nowhere. Work on making these changes in your life, so that the benefits become lasting ones.

Chapter 4

Leaving the Judgments Out of It

In the last chapter you learned how to tell the difference between your emotional, reasoning, and wise selves; you learned some ways to get to your own inner wisdom; and you learned how to reduce your vulnerability to being controlled by your emotions. In this chapter, we'll continue this last theme with another skill that will help you not be controlled by your emotions: being nonjudgmental.

Being Nonjudgmental to Quiet Intense Emotions

Most people never really notice that the words they use can actually have an effect on their emotions. When you judge, you intensify the emotions you're experiencing. Think about a time when you were annoyed, frustrated, irritated, or even angry about something, and you started to vent to someone about it. It might have gone something like this: "I can't believe he would do such a stupid thing. It never should have happened. It was the most ridiculous thing I've ever seen!"

Now think about what those judgments ("stupid," "should/shouldn't," "ridiculous") did for your emotions. Once you started venting, did you feel better? Usually, the answer is no—you don't feel better, and you actually relive the emotions you experienced when you were going through the situation for the first time, which, in other words, just makes you feel worse.

Before we get further into this and what you can do about it, let's slow down and take a look at what exactly we mean by the word "judgment," and how this works.

What Is a Judgment?

In DBT, when we talk about a judgment, we're really talking about the language we use—take the previous examples of "stupid," "should/shouldn't," and "ridiculous." These are negative judgments. Of course, people often judge in positive ways as well: "This is awesome," "You did a great job," "You're a wonderful friend," and so on—I'll say a bit more about this later on. But for now I'll just mention that because positive judgments don't increase emotional pain we're not that concerned about them, and our focus will be on the negative judgments.

Usually, the judgment that increases your pain starts with an emotion. For example, you might have a disagreement with your friend. You're feeling angry with her, and the judgments start: *She's being a total idiot*, or *She's always so mean to me*, or *She's a loser*. First of all, let me say that this is a normal human experience: our brains are judging machines, and we judge all the time! Having said that, however, it's also really not helpful for us to judge, because what happens next is that our painful emotions start to increase. We start out feeling angry, and the judgments escalate this emotion so that we're feeling even more anger, or maybe even rage, and we might start to feel other, related emotions as well—such as resentment, hurt, and bitterness.

Can you think of a time this has happened to you? A time when you started with an emotion—hurt, frustration, irritation, annoyance—and this led to your thoughts turning judgmental, which caused more emotions, which led to more judgments... and the next thing you knew, you were in your emotional self! Another way you can think about judgments is by using the term "inflammatory language." If you think of this as language that tends to incite anger and other strong emotions, we can apply this to judgmental language, and we can see how judging inflames us; it adds fuel to our emotional fire, stirring us up and creating more painful emotions.

Practicing Mindfulness to Judgments

Don't believe me? The next time something happens with a teacher at school, or you have an argument with your mom or dad, or with your brother or sister, try this: Vent to someone about it. Throw yourself into retelling the story, using judgments like you normally would, but—and this is the key here—notice what happens as you do so. Be mindful to your internal experience, noticing what happens to your emotions—do they stay the same throughout the telling of your story, do they decrease, or do they increase? What happens in your body—do you remain relaxed and calm, or do you start to tense up? What about your voice? Does it remain calm and at the same level as you tell the story, or does the volume of your voice increase as you speak? After you've finished, really pay attention to how you feel—do you feel better? Worse? The same?

By the way, researchers have shown time and again that this kind of venting actually causes a person to relive the experience, which generally means that the painful emotions increase through the telling of the story, resulting in that person actually feeling worse, not better.

The Consequences of Judging

Hopefully I've been pretty clear about the impact that judging has on your emotions: it keeps you on that roller coaster! And you may have already seen this for yourself if you've practiced being mindful to your experience when you're venting. But the increase in emotional pain is only part of the problem when it comes to judging. Let's take a look at some other ways working on reducing your judgments will help you.

Judging Makes You More Vulnerable to Your Emotional Self

The more you judge, the more emotions you have. And the more emotions you have, the harder they are to manage, and the more likely it will be that you end up acting from your emotional self.

Imagine that you have a dam within you that your emotions sit behind. The higher your emotional level, the less additional emotion it will take before the emotions overflow (and this might mean temper tantrums, meltdowns, lashing out at others, unhealthy coping, self-harming behaviors, and so on). If your emotions regularly sit at a lower level behind that dam, however, you're going to have a higher tolerance for stressful situations—you'll be more able to deal with them, rather than having your emotions burst over the dam and lead to unhealthy or unhelpful behaviors. Being nonjudgmental more often will help you keep your emotions at a more manageable level.

Judging Others Affects Relationships

You can probably recall a time (or many!) when others have judged you negatively. How did it feel? Not very good, right? Not only does it hurt and probably trigger anger, but I find it also sometimes causes people to question themselves—wondering, for example, *Am I really stupid?* Recalling how it feels when others judge you, it's obvious that when you're judging someone, this will have a negative consequence for your relationship with that person. It's hurtful. And you can't take it back, even if you realize later on that you didn't really mean it. Can you think of a time when your judging someone caused problems in your relationship?

Judging Doesn't Provide Helpful Information

The other part to the fact that judging others causes problems in your relationships is that judging doesn't provide the person with helpful information, and so it's much harder for her to try to change her behavior (if she chooses to), because she doesn't really know what the problem is! For example, let's say you do a presentation in class; afterward, the teacher tells you that it was pretty bad. Well, first of all, for most people this would be hurtful. But secondly, you don't really know what "pretty bad" means, do you? How can you do better on your next presentation when you don't know how to change it to better match the teacher's expectations? She may mean that you just aren't very effective at public speaking: you stumble a lot, you don't make eye contact, or you don't speak loud enough, for example. Or she may mean that you didn't have enough audiovisual aids, and you in fact had some information in your presentation that was inaccurate. The point here is that, in order for you to change your behavior so that it's more to your teacher's liking, you need more information than what she's given you with her judgment of "pretty bad." When you have this information, it's then up to you whether you want to make those changes or not.

Self-Judgments Damage Self-Esteem

So far we've looked at how we judge others, and we might also judge situations. But the fact is, many of us are very judgmental of ourselves as well. You may have heard the saying "We're our own worst critics." Well, this saying exists for a reason! Sometimes people will tell me they "have to" judge themselves—how else will they learn from their mistakes? Well, I guarantee that you can learn from your mistakes without judging yourself for them; and in fact, you'll be less likely to learn from your mistakes if you're judging yourself, because you're so busy beating yourself up that you can't properly assess what you could have done differently that might have been more effective—that's learning from your mistakes.

Let's look at Ashley as an example. At seventeen, she's found that she's having trouble with alcohol—she's drinking every weekend at parties with her friends, and recently she's actually started craving it during the week. Here's an example of how her self-judgmental talk might go: *I'm such a loser. I shouldn't be drinking so much on the weekends, never mind during the week. None of my friends are having this problem; what the hell is wrong with me? I'm totally screwing up my life.*

It sounds like Ashley started off feeling disappointed, or maybe even angry at herself. But these judgments likely have her feeling even more angry with herself, and probably other emotions as well, such as bitterness, fear, and sadness.

So what would happen if Ashley worked on changing her self-talk and was able to reduce (or even eliminate) her judgments? It might sound something like this: *I really don't like the fact that I've been drinking so much on the weekends, and now I'm getting worried because I'm starting to crave alcohol during the week. None of my friends are having this problem. If I keep going this way, my grades will slip and I might not be able to get into college.*

Can you see the difference here? Ashley is still looking at the mistakes she's making, and hopefully she's learning from them, but she's doing it without judging herself. Remember, judging herself would actually just increase her emotions, putting her into her emotional self, and it's much more difficult to try to problem solve when you're thinking from your emotional self.

Here's another way of thinking about self-judgments: when you're judging yourself in this way, you're verbally abusing yourself; you're bullying yourself. We all know that abusing and bullying others is *not* acceptable. So why on earth would it be acceptable to treat yourself this way? If you recognize that you're very self-judgmental, here's something for you to start working on.

When you hear the judgments arise within you (and we'll talk more in a moment about how to do this), ask yourself, *What would I say to my sister* (or best friend, mother, and so on) *if she was having this problem?* Alternatively, you could ask *What would my sister* (or best friend, mother, and so on) *say to me if she knew I was struggling with this right now?*

The bottom line is that it's not okay for other people to treat you this way, and you have to learn that it's also not okay for you to treat yourself this way.

Some Judgments Are Necessary

You might be relieved to know that, although we're talking about the importance of being aware of whenever you're judging, the point of this skill isn't to eliminate judgments. And, in fact, that would be pretty impossible. Even people who have been practicing these skills daily for many years can't be completely nonjudgmental, so that isn't the goal. With all the DBT skills, just as I mentioned with mindfulness, you're now on a path. There's no getting to the end of the path—you're never going to be *completely* mindful or *completely* nonjudgmental. But you're on the path of practicing these skills, and as time goes on you'll find that they come more naturally for you.

So no, we're not trying to get rid of judgments, but we do want to be less judgmental, and we do want to be more aware of when we're judging, so that we have the choice of whether we want to work on changing the judgment or not.

Judgments vs. Evaluations

Sometimes judgments are actually necessary, but I've come to label those judgments as "evaluations." You have to be judged at school or at work, for example—you need to be graded in order to decide if you're doing well enough in school to move on, and you need to have performance appraisals at work to ensure that you're doing what's expected of you. But in these circumstances, you're not being judged in the same way we've been using this word (your teacher isn't telling you you're "bad" at math, for example, although your grades are a short-form way of indicating this), but evaluated; for example, "Maryk is struggling with math and could benefit from coming for extra help after class."

Another example of an evaluation versus a judgment would be when you're approaching an intersection and the hand starts flashing red just as you begin to cross. Is it safe for you to continue, or do you need to turn back and wait until the next light? This is an evaluation. (A judgment would be something like *Stupid light!*)

Here's a related point: sometimes emotions don't escalate because of our judgments because the judgment didn't come from an emotion and therefore doesn't inflame us. For example, if you ever go grocery shopping with your parents, you may see one of them pick up a tomato and, assessing it as bad, put it back. Yes, "bad" is a judgment! But in this case, because the judgment didn't come from an emotion, it's similar to an evaluation in that it's not escalating the emotion.

Sometimes when I'm teaching this skill, a client will say "So this is really about semantics"—in other words, it's just about the language we use and the way we say things. And my response is *yes*! It really is just about the way we say things. But the surprising part for most people is that, by changing the way we speak (and think), we can have a positive effect on our emotions—and by working on this skill, you can help yourself get off the emotional roller coaster more often.

Positive Judgments

I mentioned earlier that we often judge in a positive way as well: "good," "right," "beautiful," "awesome," and so on. And while I mentioned that we're not as concerned with these positive judgments because they don't trigger emotional pain like negative judgments do, it's still important to be aware of them. The main reason we might not want to judge even in a positive way is that, when we're judging something or someone in a positive way, that judgment could turn into a negative under different circumstances. Let's say you bring home your report card, and your parents tell you how awesome you are for getting straight As. Well, what would it mean if your next report card had a couple of Bs, or even a C or two? Would that mean you're no longer awesome? Would it mean you're awful? Likewise, let's say you have a friend that you think is really great. If she did something you didn't like, would that turn her into a bad friend?

Another reason positive judgments can be problematic involves self-judgments. If you're a person who has habitually judged yourself, this is a tough pattern to break, and for most people with this problem, turning negative judgments into positive ones just isn't believable. Think about it: if you're used to thinking of yourself as a failure, for example, and you try to turn this into positive self-talk by reassuring yourself that you're really a success, chances are you'll give up on this because you just don't buy it.

So the best idea is to try to steer clear of judgments—negative and positive—more often. With that, let's turn to look at how you can actually practice this skill.

What to Do About Judgments

First, I want to make sure you understand that expressing yourself nonjudgmentally is still expressing yourself. This is not about stuffing your emotions or keeping your opinions to yourself. And in fact, as you'll soon see, being nonjudgmental is really a way of being more assertive. But I'm jumping ahead; let's break this down into steps so you know exactly what you need to do.

Increasing Awareness

As with any behavior, you can't work on changing something until you first work on increasing your awareness of it. Chances are, having simply read about this skill, you're now going to be more aware of when you're judging—whether yourself, others, situations, or something else. But keep in mind that judgments often happen so automatically (in part because it's what we've learned from our families, our friends, and society as a whole) that you might find it difficult to even notice when you're judging.

Let's look at a mindfulness exercise that will help you increase your awareness of your judgments. Practicing this exercise regularly will help you become more aware of your judgmental thoughts, as well as of your thoughts and emotions in a more general sense.

Exercise: The Gatekeeper

Sitting in a comfortable position, pay attention to your breath. Breathe in, breathe out—slowly, deeply, and comfortably. As you breathe, allow yourself to notice any sensations you're experiencing—the feel of the air as it enters your nostrils, passes down your throat, and fills your lungs, and then as you exhale, the feel of your lungs deflating, as the air passes back out through your nose or mouth.

After a few moments of focusing on your breath, draw your attention to your thoughts and emotions. Imagine that you are standing at the door of a castle wall. You're the gatekeeper, in charge of who comes and goes through that doorway. What comes through the door isn't people, but your thoughts and feelings. The idea here, though, isn't that you get to decide which thoughts and feelings come in—if they come to the door, they need to be let in, or they'll just camp outside that door and continue to bang on it harder and harder. Instead, the idea is that you greet each thought and feeling as it enters, just acknowledging its presence before the next thought or feeling arrives. In other words, you accept each experience as it comes—*A judgmental thought is at the door*; *Here is anger*; *Here is a judgmental thought about myself*; *This is sadness*; and so on.

By your acknowledging your thoughts and emotions, each of these experiences will pass through the door and continue on their way rather than stick around. The thought or emotion might come back again and again, but you'll see that it doesn't stay long; it just passes through, and then the next experience arises.

Turning a Judgment into a Nonjudgment

Once you're noticing the judgments more often (and this will take time and practice), you can start working on changing your judgments to neutral or nonjudgmental statements. And by the way, when I talk about these statements, I'm referring to both the thoughts that go through your head and the ones that you say out loud; there's no difference.

First, it's important for you to understand that this isn't about changing a negative judgment to a positive one—remember that ideally you don't want to be judging in a positive way either, for the most part. Instead, the idea is to take the judgment out altogether and replace it with a nonjudgmental or neutral statement. Let's take a look at the formula I use for this.

* State the facts.

   Identify the judgmental word and take it out of your sentence. Replace the judgment with the facts. Stating the facts means exactly that: you're not judging, interpreting, or making assumptions; instead, you're stating the facts exactly as you know them.

* Express your emotion(s).

   The second part to this formula is expressing your feelings about the situation: what was the emotion that arose within you that caused you to want to judge in the first place?

Now let's look at an example: You've made plans to go to the movies with your friend on Saturday night. That morning, your friend calls and tells you she's been asked out on a date, so she can't go to the movies with you. Your automatic, judgmental thought might be something like this: *Oh sure, she gets a better offer and dumps me. What a jerk. Some friend she is.* In other words, you're judging her as a bad friend. So let's use our formula to change this to a nonjudgmental statement:

* State the facts.

  My friend got asked out on a date and canceled the plans we had made last week.

* Express your emotion(s).

  I feel really hurt and angry.

If you put these statements together, you get this nonjudgmental statement: *I feel hurt and angry because my friend got asked out on a date and canceled the plans we had made last week.* This is a clear statement that isn't judgmental, so it isn't going to escalate your emotions, and yet it still gets across the emotions you're feeling. Essentially, this is an assertive way of communicating. If you were to say this to your friend, she would have no reason to feel judged, and yet she would understand how you felt and why. She would then be able to change her behavior if she chose to, because you've provided her with the information she needs about how her behavior affected you.

Let's look at one more example: You're going for your driver's test. You've been working hard, practicing every day after school for weeks. Passing is really important to you, and you're feeling confident about your skills. The day comes, you take your test, and all goes well—you know you've aced it. However, once you pull into the parking lot and finish your test, your examiner begins explaining to you why you've failed. Your judgmental thought might be something like this: *What an idiot! I can't believe he just failed me. He obviously doesn't know what the hell he's doing. This is crazy!*

So again, let's break this down so that you're taking the judgment out and not experiencing more emotions than you should be.

* State the facts.

   The examiner just failed me even though I believe I did really well.

* Express your emotion(s).

   I'm really angry with the examiner, and I'm also hugely disappointed that I didn't get my license today.

The nonjudgmental statement therefore becomes *I'm really angry with the examiner for failing me because I thought I did really well, and I'm hugely disappointed that I didn't get my license today.*

Remember, this skill isn't going to take the emotions away. So when you're nonjudgmental about your friend who canceled your plans at the last minute, you're still going to feel hurt. And when you're nonjudgmental about the examiner who failed you on your driving test, you're still going to feel angry and disappointed. None of the skills you're learning here are going to get rid of your emotions. That's impossible and not our goal. What this skill and the others you'll learn in this book will do is help you not escalate your emotions, and when you're not increasing your emotions they're often much more manageable. In this way, over time, you'll learn to bear your pain more skillfully.

Your Next Steps

In this chapter you've learned about being nonjudgmental, and how this will help you survive the roller coaster you've been on. This is a skill that takes a lot of practice—remember, it's going to take a lot of practice for most people just to become aware of when they are judging. So that's where you start: practice the Gatekeeper exercise outlined in this chapter to help increase your awareness of your thoughts, which will help you become more aware of the judgments when they arise, and help increase your awareness of other things we'll be working on later in this book.

You might also consider sharing at least some of the information you're learning in this book with someone you trust so that she or he can help you practice these skills; for example, it can make things easier if you have someone pointing out to you (in a supportive rather than a judgmental way!) when you're judging. Making it a team effort can help you catch your judgments more often.

The second part to practice, of course, is when you notice a judgment, turning it into a neutral or nonjudgmental statement. Please understand that, for most people, this takes a lot of practice; it's not something that comes naturally. Remember that everyone around you is judging pretty constantly, so the judgments come automatically. But once you can get off that automatic pilot more often and reduce the negative judgments, you'll notice that you're experiencing fewer moments of being caught up in your emotional self, and you'll be able to manage your emotions more effectively as a result. So please practice!

In the next chapter, you're going to learn another skill that will help quiet your intense emotions and that actually adds to a nonjudgmental stance, so make sure you have a fairly good understanding of this skill before you move on to chapter 5. That doesn't mean you need to have mastered this skill, of course—remember that this is a journey you're on; there is no mastering!

Chapter 5

Dealing with Intense Emotions

In the last chapter you learned about how judgments can actually increase your emotional load, and that, by changing your judgmental thoughts to nonjudgmental or neutral statements, you can actually reduce the amount of emotional pain you're experiencing. In this chapter, we're going to continue with this theme of reducing the intensity of emotions to make them more bearable by practicing self-validation—essentially, practicing being nonjudgmental with emotions. When your emotions are less intense, you'll have more ability to manage them, which over time will help you get off the emotional roller coaster.

Messages About Emotions

Let's start by having you think about the messages you've received about emotions. We all receive these messages, from family, close friends, and peers, and from society as a whole. Let's take a look at some examples so you have a better idea of what I mean.

"Anger Is Bad"

One message that's quite common is that anger is a bad emotion, or that if you feel angry, you're a bad person for feeling that way (remember, "bad" is a judgment). In other words, you shouldn't (and "shoulds" and "shouldn'ts" are almost always judgments) feel angry. There are lots of ways people might come to believe this. For example, if you have a parent who explodes with anger—or perhaps has even been verbally, emotionally, or physically abusive—you might have grown up being afraid of anger, and this has influenced you to believe that anger is a bad emotion.

Or you may have a family who believes that anger is bad, and so whenever someone in your family expresses anger, they're given this message in some way: they shouldn't feel angry. Maybe they're being silly (judgment!) for being angry, or you or your siblings may have been sent to your rooms because you were expressing anger. You may also have grown up seeing your parents or other caregivers stuffing their anger—not expressing it, or pretending they didn't feel angry—and this can also send the message that anger is an emotion that's not okay to feel.

"Don't Worry"

You may have heard these words when you're feeling anxious or nervous about something. Take your parent, for example, who may have told you as a child that you were being silly for being afraid of the dark or of the monster under your bed. Although this is usually meant to be reassuring, when you hear it often enough, you may take it as a message that you shouldn't be feeling this way: you shouldn't be worrying, there's really no reason for you to worry, you're being silly or ridiculous (more judgments), and so on.

"There's Nothing for You to Feel Sad About"

Similarly, have you ever been asked why you feel sad and told that "there's nothing for you to feel sad about"? So the message is that you shouldn't feel sad. Again, judgment. Just because there is no discernable reason for your sadness or depression doesn't mean you shouldn't feel that way. And the more people question why you feel this way, the more likely you are to question it and judge it yourself: *What's wrong with me? There's no reason for me to feel this way.*

I mentioned earlier that we also receive messages about emotions from our peers. If you think for a moment, you can probably come up with some of these on your own. One example is kids daring each other to do things, and if they don't, they're "chicken," which sends the message that being afraid of something is negative in some way; for example, it makes you weak. Similarly, a common message in society is that boys shouldn't cry, but that's it's okay for girls to show emotion in this way.

These are just a few examples of the messages you might have received about some painful emotions. Let's look now at why this is important, and how it might be fueling your roller coaster ride.

How Your Beliefs Affect the Way You Feel: Primary vs. Secondary Emotions

Over time, you come to internalize the messages you've received about emotions, and as you can see, these messages often have consequences for how you feel about your emotions. So if you've grown up in a family where it's not acceptable to feel anger, for example, you'll probably believe when you feel angry that you shouldn't feel it. Or if you've learned from your peers that anxiety or sadness makes you weak, you might believe that having these feelings means you're a weak person, and you'll do everything you can to avoid feeling this way. And this is where the problem lies: when you have negative judgments about the emotion you're experiencing, it actually increases your emotional pain, because you're judging yourself for having the emotions. Also, people often then try to avoid the emotion, suppress it, or push it away, and this leads to all sorts of other problems; for example, you might continuously stuff your anger until finally one day you explode, or you may turn to drinking alcohol or using drugs to try to avoid feeling the pain you're in. Welcome to the emotional roller coaster.

Before we get to the question of what to do about this, you need a bit more information about emotions. You may recall from chapter 2 that we don't generally have an emotional reaction in response to a situation, but that our emotion usually arises in response to our interpretation of a situation. A *primary emotion* is the emotion that comes up first, in response to your interpretation of a situation, and a *secondary emotion* is the emotion that comes up in response to your primary emotion. Essentially, a secondary emotion is how you feel about your feelings.

It's important that you understand the difference between these two types of emotions, because it's the primary emotion that you're going to use the skill of validation with. By validating the primary emotion, you won't have the secondary emotions to deal with. So let's look at an example.

✳ *Percy's Story*

Percy grew up with a father who didn't understand his anxiety and who was hard on Percy whenever he expressed anxiety. This of course didn't help Percy's anxiety, and it resulted in his believing that he shouldn't feel anxious, which actually made him more anxious at times, as well as triggering frustration and anger at himself for feeling this way. Here's how it would go: Percy would encounter a situation that made him anxious; for example, meeting new people. The thought would be something like What if they don't like me or I make an idiot of myself? *He would start to feel anxious in response to his thoughts about the situation (the primary emotion), and then his judgmental thoughts would kick in:* This is so stupid. I shouldn't be anxious about this. No one else feels anxious about situations like these; what's wrong with me? What if I never get over this? *These judgmental thoughts would then trigger Percy's secondary emotions: he'd start to feel angry at himself and maybe ashamed for feeling anxious, and he'd also feel more anxious because he'd be thinking there was something wrong with him, and he'd be worrying that he'd never get over his anxiety.*

103

So in this example, Percy's primary emotion is anxiety, and his secondary emotions include anger at himself, shame, and more anxiety. Take some time to do the following exercise to help you become more familiar with how to identify your own primary emotions.

Exercise: Identifying Your Primary Emotion

For this exercise, you'll need to think of a recent time when you experienced an intense emotion. Perhaps you became angry with a parent or friend, or maybe you felt sad, hurt, or frustrated about a difficult situation. Do your best to put yourself back in that situation and feel the emotions that were coming up for you; it may help if you close your eyes.

Once you have a good memory of the situation, as best as you can, focus on what emotions came up for you. Can you name them? If you can't, try going back to chapter 2 to review the emotions listed there, along with some of the alternate words for those emotions, and the situations in which those emotions would be expected to arise. Then you can come back to your situation and see if you can put a name on the emotions you were experiencing at the time.

Once you can name the emotions you were experiencing, see if you can identify the thoughts that were triggering that emotion.

For example, Percy noticed the thought *What if they don't like me?* and connected this to his anxiety, a fear related to a possible future scenario ("what-ifs"). He also noticed the thought *There's something wrong with me for feeling anxious about this,* and he recognized that this was a judgmental thought that was triggering a secondary emotion: anger at himself for feeling anxious.

The easiest way to tell the difference between your primary emotions and your secondary emotions is to look at the thoughts triggering those emotions: the thoughts that are related to the situation (for example, *What if they don't like me?*) will trigger primary emotions, and the thoughts that are related to your emotional experience (for example, *There's something wrong with me for feeling anxious about this*) will trigger secondary emotions.

And actually, here's a general tip: if you're feeling guilty about the emotions you're experiencing, you're judging yourself. Remember, emotions are never wrong—how you're feeling is how you should be feeling, given your current circumstances and interpretations of the situation. So if you're experiencing guilt for feeling angry, for example, there is some kind of judgmental thought going on. Likewise, if you're feeling the need to push a feeling away, avoid or escape it, or ignore it in some way, you're judging it.

Now that you've got a better idea about how judging your (primary) emotions will trigger more (secondary) emotional pain, what can you do to help interrupt this cycle so that you're no longer triggering extra emotional pain for yourself? I've already mentioned that this is about being nonjudgmental with your feelings; this is a skill known as self-validation.

Validating Your Emotions

Validating your emotions is basically being nonjudgmental with your emotions. It's accepting whatever emotion is there—not saying that you like it, but being neutral or nonjudgmental toward it and toward yourself for having it. And, just like with a nonjudgmental stance, when you can validate your emotion, you prevent the emotion from escalating. Bear in mind that this is yet another skill that doesn't aim to get rid of your emotions—remember, that's not the goal with DBT. But the more you can reduce your emotional intensity, the more able you'll be to manage the emotions that are present for you. So how do you do this?

You probably won't be surprised to hear that the first step to validating your emotions is to become aware of when you're judging them. Mindfulness in general—and specifically the Gatekeeper exercise you learned in chapter 4—will help with this, so hopefully you've been practicing this exercise and becoming more aware of your judgments, as well as of your thoughts and emotions overall. Once you become aware that you're judging yourself for an emotion you're experiencing, you'll be able to work on validating yourself.

Remember, invalidating is when you're judging yourself for the emotions you're experiencing, so when it comes to self-validating, you want to stop the judgments and be more accepting of your emotional experience. There are a few ways of doing this.

Acknowledging

The first way of validating yourself is by acknowledging what the experience is. By simply labeling or naming the emotion—*This is anxiety* or *I feel angry*, for example—you're validating the emotion just by the fact that you're no longer judging it. This is the most basic way of validating, but it's still very effective. Think of Percy once again; if he had been able to acknowledge his anxiety rather than judging it the way he did, he wouldn't have had all the secondary emotions pop up.

Now think back to the situation you recalled in the previous exercise: how would you acknowledge your primary emotion in that scenario?

Allowing

Allowing an emotion takes validation a step further, because you're giving yourself permission to feel the feeling. So, instead of *I feel anxious*, the self-talk becomes *It's okay that I feel anxious*, or *I'm allowed to feel this way*. Let's be clear that this isn't saying you like the feeling or that you're not going to make efforts to change the feeling; it's just acknowledging that this is a normal human emotion, and that sometimes people feel this way—it's not the end of the world, and it doesn't mean anything about you as a person. Again, going back to the situation you were visualizing earlier in the chapter, what might you say to yourself that would allow your primary emotion?

Understanding

Validating your emotion by understanding it takes this one step further again, by giving the emotion context. In other words, you're saying that you understand why you feel the way you feel in that moment, that it makes sense given the circumstances and situation. To go back to Percy, for example, he might be able to say to himself, *It makes sense that I feel anxious when I meet new people because I was bullied as a kid, and it's hard for me to trust others now.* So, going back to that situation you were visualizing one last time, can you validate your primary emotion from this perspective? I do need to point out that Percy might not actually know why he feels anxious when he meets new people. And that's okay—we don't always know where our emotions come from. If you can't validate your emotion in this way because you don't understand it, you can still acknowledge it or allow it. Remember, as long as you're not judging yourself for feeling the feeling, you're validating it.

Now let's look at a mindfulness exercise that will help you change your attitude toward yourself and your emotions, which in turn will help you be more validating in the long run. You'll start the practice by directing compassion toward yourself, and as this starts to come more naturally for you, you will then start to extend these kind thoughts to others as well. If it's more difficult for you to turn compassion toward yourself, you can start with compassion toward others and work your way back to yourself as it becomes more comfortable.

Exercise: Loving-Kindness Meditation

Find a place to sit in a comfortable position. Once you're settled, bring your attention to your breathing. You don't have to change how you're breathing; just notice how it feels to breathe. Then, gradually as you inhale and exhale, you can begin to regulate your breathing, so that you're breathing slowly, deeply, and comfortably.

As you continue to focus on your breath, allow yourself to connect with positive emotions—feelings of kindness, friendliness, warmth, and compassion. These are the feelings you experience as you greet someone you really care for, when your pet greets you with unconditional love, or when you do something nice for someone. Let your memory drift to a time when you experienced that warmth and kindness toward someone. Allow those feelings to come into the present moment, and let yourself feel the joy, love, and other positive feelings that come up for you. As you experience these feelings of compassion, love, kindness, and friendliness, gently say the following phrases to yourself, directing them toward yourself:

May I be happy.

May I be healthy.

May I be peaceful.

May I be safe.

You can either think these statements to yourself or say them out loud; either way, as best as you can, really feel the words as you say them—putting feeling and meaning into each phrase as you say it. If you have a hard time directing these feelings of kindness toward yourself, remember that habits take time to change. In other words, don't judge yourself or the exercise; just know that this is something you'll need to spend more time on. Practice this exercise regularly, and you'll find that you're able to take a more kind, loving, and gentle attitude toward yourself and others, which will help you be more validating and accepting of your own experience and less judgmental of yourself and others.

Your Next Steps

Although you're learning many skills in this book that are probably pretty new to you, you might have noticed that these skills are quite interconnected: mindfulness includes acceptance, which is being nonjudgmental, and validation is being non-judgmental with your emotions, for example. So if you get overwhelmed, slow down (remember, I want you to work your way through this book slowly anyway, really working on understanding and implementing the skills you're reading about). Go back to just one thing: perhaps mindfulness, since it's the basis for so many of the other skills you're learning. Or maybe you've found one skill that really resonates for you right now—focus on just that one skill. When things settle down a bit for you, you can turn back to the other skills. But the main thing is that in some way, you're working on making these skills a part of your life.

In this chapter you've learned how to validate your emotions. Remember that it always starts with awareness—you can't change a behavior until you're aware of what's happening, so make sure you continue to practice your mindfulness in a variety of ways. Noticing when your emotions seem to be stronger than what you think is warranted by the current situation is usually a good indicator that judgments are happening, so when you notice this, turn your attention to your thoughts and try to notice if you're judging yourself for your emotions. And practice the loving-kindness meditation. It's a wonderful way of working on increasing your compassion toward yourself and others—and heaven knows we could all use a little more compassion in this world!

When you're feeling ready, you can move on to the next chapter, where we'll be looking at skills that will help you be more effective in your life, which will result in fewer intense emotions.

Chapter 6

Stop Letting
Your Emotions
Get in the Way

How often do you look back on a decision you've made, or something you've done, and feel regret about that decision or behavior? How often do you wish that you had done things differently? The DBT skill of being effective is about learning to act in ways that help you move toward your long-term goals, and in ways you won't regret later on. In chapter 5, you learned about the skill of self-validation, which will reduce the extent to which your emotions get in the way and is in itself being effective. In this chapter, you'll learn other ways to help you be more effective in moving toward your goals, and you'll learn a skill that will help you do something other than what your emotions are telling you to do, which will also help you move in that direction.

What Does It Mean to Be Effective?

Being effective means different things to different people, and different things in different situations. It means weighing your reasoning with your emotions, considering long-term consequences, and acting from your wise self in order to get your needs met. Being effective means doing what works and what moves you closer to your long-term goals. That, of course, means first of all figuring out what your long-term goals are, and then determining what will be most likely to help you reach those goals.

Considering Your Goals

Figuring out what your goal is—what it is that you're trying to accomplish—means deciding what's most important to you long-term, rather than short-term, and then figuring out what you might do or how you could act that will increase your chances of reaching that goal. Of course, acting effectively doesn't guarantee that you'll get your needs met, but it will increase your chances of getting what you're after in the situation.

"Don't Cut Off Your Nose to Spite Your Face"

You might have heard the saying "Don't cut off your nose to spite your face." As odd as this saying sounds, it's referring to the times when you do something that might feel good or give you satisfaction in the moment but goes against your best interests in the long run, because it's not moving you closer to your goal. Usually, this means you're acting from your emotional self. Cutting off your nose to spite your face (or "shooting yourself in the foot" does the trick too!) is the opposite of being effective. Being effective means acting from your inner wisdom, taking into consideration how you feel, what you think, and what your intuition is telling you will be in your best long-term interest.

Acting from Your Wise Self

Of course, while being effective is about doing what it takes to meet your goals, this doesn't give you free rein to do so at the expense of others. Remember that being effective comes from your wisdom, and so it's also about acting in ways that match your morals and values. Otherwise, you'll end up losing self-respect, which is obviously not in your best interest!

Let's take a look at an example.

✳ Nick's Story

Nick was determined to get into his first choice of college. He had a plan for his future that included becoming a veterinarian, and he knew which school he wanted to go to in order to achieve this plan and be successful. Nick was doing volunteer work at a local animal shelter and was counting on a great reference from the director, but a couple of months into his work there, he began having problems with the supervisor. He didn't feel that she was treating him fairly in giving him the cleanup jobs more often than the other volunteers. Nick also felt like his supervisor had taken a dislike to him for some reason. She didn't speak to him often, he felt like she avoided him, and when she did speak with him, it seemed to be with a tone of voice that indicated her dislike and disdain for him.

Nick couldn't understand why the supervisor was treating him this way, and it was making him increasingly unhappy and uncomfortable. It was getting to the point that he didn't look forward to his volunteer work anymore. Wanting to stay at the shelter to put in his hours, get his reference, and learn more about animals, Nick decided that what would be most effective would be to try speaking with the supervisor; if that didn't work, he would go to the director and ask if it would be possible to switch shifts, even though the scheduled hours would be less convenient for him.

Why was this effective? What Nick probably felt like doing was lashing right back at the supervisor—it sucks when someone isn't treating you the way you'd like and you feel as though there's nothing you can do about it. You might even be thinking Nick *wasn't* effective—that he should have talked back to the supervisor or even quit his volunteer position. But remember what Nick's long-term goal is: to become a veterinarian. He accessed his inner wisdom to consider what would be most likely to help him reach this goal, and volunteering at the local shelter was the thing his gut told him he needed to do, not just for his résumé but also for the hands-on experience. Leaving the shelter would have been cutting off his nose to spite his face—it might have felt good in the short run to tell the supervisor where to go and to quit, but doing so certainly wouldn't have helped Nick move in the direction of his goal.

Hopefully this is starting to make a little more sense to you. And once it does, you'll probably see that many of the skills we've looked at so far will help you be more effective, especially if your goal is to survive the emotional roller coaster! But before we start looking at skills to help with this, it's important that you take some time to think about how effective you are (or aren't) in your life already. Can you think of a time when you've shot yourself in the foot? When you've allowed your emotional self to take over and get in the way of reaching your long-term goals? Do you think this is something that happens regularly for you? Keep in mind that we all act ineffectively sometimes. But if this is a regular occurrence for you, it's something you'll really need to focus on.

Later in this chapter we'll look at some of the reasons that being effective can be difficult. For now, consider areas in your life where you've been able to be effective, and where you haven't. Being aware of these instances can help you see what you might need to work on. It can also be helpful if you think about what you have going on in your life right now where this skill will be helpful. If you can think of some current or near-future situations, keep those in mind as you read through the rest of this chapter, and see what ideas you can apply to those situations.

Let's turn now to another skill that will help you be more effective in managing your emotions.

Acting Opposite to Your Emotion

A specific skill that can help you be more effective is the DBT skill of acting opposite to your emotion. When you're using this skill, you start by identifying the emotion you're experiencing (such as anxiety about doing a presentation in class). Next you identify the urge that's attached to the emotion (for example, you might be considering avoiding—you could easily skip class today), and then you act opposite to what the emotion is telling you to do (instead of skipping class, you push yourself to go and get the presentation over with).

So in the earlier example with Nick, it might go something like this: Nick identifies that he's feeling angry at his supervisor for the way she's been treating him. The urge associated with the anger would probably be to lash out at her, perhaps yelling at her and trying to make her see that she's being really awful to him. To act opposite to what his emotion is telling him to do, Nick might try to avoid being around her for a little while so he'll be less triggered and more able to deal with this in a way that will be effective for him. In other words, Nick recognizes that lashing out at her isn't what's going to help him move toward his goals.

The following chart will help you think about how this would work for some of the painful emotions you probably experience on a regular basis:

Emotion	Urge	Opposite Action
Anger	To attack (either verbally or physically)	To leave the situation; to avoid the person; or if these aren't options, to act civilly, so you're not making things worse
Sadness	To withdraw from people; to hide away and isolate yourself	To spend time with others; to ask for help and support
Anxiety	To leave or escape the situation that's causing anxiety, and to avoid that same (and similar) situations in the future	To put yourself in or remain in the anxiety-provoking situation, and to place yourself in that situation again in the future
Guilt/Shame	To withdraw from others and hide; to stop the behavior or make up for it in some way (for example, by apologizing)	To approach others, and when guilt or shame is not justified (see chapter 2 for a discussion on these emotions), to keep doing the activity that triggers these feelings and not apologize or try to make up for it

I also need to mention here that, with the emotions of anger, guilt, and shame, using this skill means not just acting opposite to the urges to *act* that are attached to the emotion, but also doing your best to *think* opposite to the thoughts attached to the emotion. When you're feeling angry, for example, and you might be experiencing urges to lash out at someone verbally or physically, or perhaps to throw something, there's something else that's keeping the anger going: your thoughts. And if you look closely at those thoughts, you'll probably realize that they're judgmental thoughts. You might remember from chapter 4 that judgments add fuel to the emotional fire; for example, when you're angry at your mother and you judge her (*She's always so mean to me*), this judgment keeps your anger going. Or when you're feeling ashamed of yourself, your self-judgments (*I'm such an awful person*) cause more feelings of shame.

So when you're practicing the skill of acting opposite to your emotion with anger, you have to avoid the situation or person triggering the anger, or act civilly in that situation so as to not make things worse, but you also have to work on changing your judgmental thinking to nonjudgmental thinking (see chapter 4 if you need to review how to do this), in order to help reduce your anger.

Likewise with guilt and shame, the judgmental thoughts are there, but they're turned inward and we judge ourselves: *I shouldn't have done that; I'm a complete idiot; I'm a bad person;* and so on. So when unwarranted guilt and shame arise (or are ongoing and getting in your way), and you're trying to act opposite to what the emotions are telling you to do, stop hiding or trying to make up for the behavior. Continue to do the activity triggering the emotion if it's unwarranted; *and* practice being nonjudgmental toward yourself.

It's important to know that acting opposite to your emotion isn't about avoiding your emotions; remember, our goal here is to get you feeling your feelings and bearing your pain more skillfully, not to get rid of the emotions completely! Rather, this is a skill that you can use when you recognize that it's not effective for you to continue feeling a specific emotion so intensely. You might remember from chapter 2 that all emotions serve a purpose; they have jobs to do. But when an emotion has come and done its job, delivered its message—in other words, you know how you feel about a situation and you're ready to do something about it—sometimes the emotion sticking around gets in the way of your being able to do what might be most effective in that situation. We all know that when an emotion remains intense, it's hard to get to your wise self and to act in healthy, helpful ways. For example, if you're feeling really anxious about doing that presentation in class, the anxiety will probably get in the way of your getting a good grade. Or, to go back to Nick's example, if his anger remains intense, it's going to be much more difficult for him to have a productive conversation with his supervisor. So the thing to keep in mind with this skill is that if the emotion you're experiencing is no longer helping and you want to reduce it, then act opposite to what the emotion is telling you to do.

Obstacles to Effectiveness

So what makes it so difficult to act in effective ways sometimes? A number of things can get in the way of your being effective, and being aware of these can help you identify when this is occurring, so you can figure out what to do about it.

Not Knowing What Your Goal Is

Strange as this may sound, people often don't know exactly what it is they want in a situation. And obviously, if you don't know what your goal is, it will be very difficult for you to figure out what you can do to achieve it. So slow down, take some time, and give this some thought before acting. Sometimes at least part of the problem is that you might have more than one goal. Nick, for example, wants a good reference letter for school, but he also wants an enjoyable experience and to gain knowledge about working with animals. Sometimes these goals might conflict (for example, Nick might not be able to really enjoy the experience working at the shelter if he and the supervisor continue to butt heads), and when this happens, you need to access your wise self to help you decide which goal is most important to you if it's likely that you won't be able to meet them all. Nick, for example, is already considering changing shifts even though it will make life a little more difficult for him; he might also consider whether moving to another shelter is an option.

Not Responding to Reality

Another reason you may have a hard time being effective in a situation is because you're not responding to the situation as it is, but rather to your judgments about the situation and to your thoughts about the way you think the situation should be or the way you wish it was. In other words, it's your thoughts about the situation—for example, *It's not fair*; *It's wrong*; or *It shouldn't be happening*—that are getting in the way of your being effective.

To go back once more to Nick's situation, if he gets stuck thinking that his supervisor "shouldn't" be treating him this way, or that the director "should" see what's happening, these thoughts are likely to get in the way of Nick's acting effectively. As long as he's stuck in these judgmental thoughts, he's unlikely to act to change the situation. So in order to be effective, you have to respond to the situation as it is, rather than how you think it should be or how you wish it was. Here's another way to think about this: is it more important for you to be right, or for you to reach your goal?

Not Looking at the Long Run

A final thing that often gets in the way of being effective is that we have a tendency to focus on the immediate future, and this can impair our ability to think about what will be most helpful in the long run. This is essentially our emotional self getting in the way. For example, while Nick might get short-term satisfaction out of being disrespectful to his supervisor, in the long run he's likely to lose his position at the shelter, he might not get his reference letter if he can't find another shelter to volunteer at, and he's not getting the valuable experience he was hoping to gain.

So remember: in order to be effective in a situation, you must be able to get to your wise self to determine first of all what your goal is, and then what you can do to increase the likelihood that you will meet your goal. Don't cut off your nose to spite your face!

What Does This Skill Mean for You?

Now that you hopefully have a good understanding of the skill of effectiveness, you can start to think about what this skill means for your life. Do you think you have a tendency to cut off your nose to spite your face? Do you often act from your emotional self, reacting from your emotions and thinking about your short-term satisfaction rather than choosing how you can act that might move you toward your longer-term goals? Do you tend to do what feels right in the moment, rather than thinking about what the consequences of your behavior might be? What do you need to start doing differently in your life in order to be more effective?

The following mindfulness exercise will help you access your inner wisdom more often, which will increase your ability to be more effective.

Exercise: Accessing Your Wise Self

Sitting in a comfortable position, begin by bringing your focus to your breath. Breathing slowly, deeply, and comfortably, allow yourself to be open to your present experience, whatever it is. Notice any physical sensations, thoughts, or emotions that are present for you in this moment, without judgment; just allow yourself to sense whatever your current experience is. If you notice yourself getting caught up thinking about your experience rather than just observing it, bring yourself back to the anchor of your breath. When you're feeling centered and ready, ask yourself, *What would my wise self do?* Allow yourself some time to experience a response to this question; if none comes, bring acceptance to this and ask the question again. Whenever you find yourself distracted, getting caught up in thoughts or emotions, as best as you can, use your breath as an anchor to keep bringing you back to the present.

You might be surprised in doing this exercise how often your wise self will present an answer to you!

Your Next Steps

This chapter has introduced the skill of being effective in your life, as well as acting opposite to your emotion as one means of increasing your ability to be effective. Of course, all the skills you've learned so far in this book will help increase your effectiveness, but remember that it's important for you to consider what your goals are, so that you can begin to determine what steps you might take that will bring you closer to those goals.

What do you need to change in your life to be more effective? What's one small step you can take in that direction? These are really your next steps—in addition to continuing to practice mindfulness and the other skills you've learned so far, consider what effectiveness will look like for you at this point in your life. If you have difficulty setting goals for yourself, we'll be taking a closer look at this in chapter 9, so feel free to jump ahead if you need to. Or pace yourself by continuing to think about what this will look like for you, and work on goal setting when you get there. In the meantime, keep practicing!

Chapter 7

Accepting Reality

In the last couple of chapters we've been focusing on acceptance: looking at using less judgmental language and being more accepting of your emotional experience, in addition to the acceptance practice inherent in mindfulness. In addition, we've been looking at how to be more effective in your life in a variety of ways. Remember that the purpose of these skills is to help reduce the amount of emotional pain in your life, which in the long run will help you survive the emotional roller coaster. In this chapter, we'll continue to look at skills that will help you be more accepting—and therefore more effective—but this time on a broader scale, with a skill called *reality acceptance*.

What Does Fighting Reality Mean?

Let's start by looking at the opposite of accepting reality, which is fighting reality. Fighting reality is when you fall into the trap of judging the situation you're dealing with, whether it's something that's happening in your present or something that took place in your past. The important thing to remember is that you're human; and as humans, our tendency is to try to fight, avoid, ignore, and push away the things that cause us pain. But in doing so, we actually increase the pain we're experiencing, by creating suffering for ourselves. Let's go through a simple exercise to get you thinking about where this fits into your life.

Exercise: What Does Fighting Reality Look Like for You?

Start by thinking of a time when you were fighting reality. It could be any painful situation—even one you're currently fighting; for example, the person you have feelings for doesn't feel the same way about you; your parents have just told you they're separating; they're already divorced and one of them is remarrying; or you didn't get into the school you really wanted. (Generally, the more painful the situation, the more difficult it is to accept.) So pick one, and think about it for a minute. Think about how you talked to yourself about the situation, maybe saying things like *It's not fair*; *It shouldn't have happened*; *It's ridiculous* (or awful or stupid, and so on); or *It shouldn't be this way*.

Next, think about this: When you started fighting the reality, how did you feel? You might have noticed, for example, that you got more and more angry as you thought about the situation in this way. Now consider what you did: Did you vent to someone about it? Did you yell and scream to yourself in your bedroom? Did you cry? Maybe you tried to distract yourself in unhealthy ways—you ended up gaming for eight hours, or you went out with friends and decided it was a good time to experiment with drugs. Maybe you didn't know how to cope, and you ended up lashing out at the people who care about you, or you did other things you later regretted. Now consider this: Were there any benefits to fighting the reality? Did it help you in some way?

Did it reduce the pain you were feeling? Was it effective in helping you cope? How about the negative consequences—can you identify them? Were the behaviors you engaged in harmful to you, or to the people you care about?

Ideally, you now have an idea of how fighting reality affects your own life. Next, let's take a closer look at how it affects us in general.

Pain vs. Suffering

There's a saying that goes something like this: "The pain in life is inevitable, but suffering is optional," and in DBT we look at suffering as what happens when we refuse to accept the pain in our lives. In other words, we cannot avoid the pain in life: your feelings aren't returned; you don't get asked to prom (or the person you ask says no); you fail your driver's test; you don't get into the school you want; you lose a really important friendship. All these things will cause pain.

Suffering comes when you refuse to accept a situation as it is—when you fight the reality, as we looked at earlier. Suffering is the additional pain that arises when you get stuck in judging the situation, and this additional pain makes it more difficult for you to cope and to continue to function as you normally would. It often results in those unhealthy behaviors you may have a tendency to fall into, as you try to escape through sleeping, gaming, using drugs or alcohol, and so on. Let's look at an example to help you understand this idea.

✳ Carly's Story

Carly had been best friends with Roy since the very start of first grade. They lived right down the street from each other, so they would walk to school together and play together on weekends. Over the summer, their families would spend time together as well. When the two friends started high school, however, Roy met some new people and things began to change. Roy stopped walking home from school with Carly and started getting rides with some of his new friends instead, never offering to ask if Carly could join them. Gradually, Carly realized that Roy wasn't returning her calls or texts all the time, and she was having to search him out at school. Also, when she would find him, he didn't seem to want to talk much or spend time with her. Finally, one day when Carly approached Roy while he was with his new friends, he said some really hurtful things, called her a loser, and laughed at her with his friends.

Carly, of course, was really hurt, and she was angry at Roy for humiliating her in front of his friends. She couldn't believe that this was the person she had grown up with. She went home early that day, went straight to her room, and lay down on the bed. Thinking about the situation, Carly's experience went something like this: I can't believe he's being so awful. What's wrong with him? We've been friends for so long, and he shouldn't be treating me this way. *(Carly's anger starts to increase with her judgments.)* That stupid jerk. *(She starts to cry.)* He's such a loser. I should never have been friends with him in the first place. *(She becomes more and more angry and starts to sob.)*

Having difficulties dealing with the pain, Carly starts to think about ways she might numb herself. Her parents have a fully stocked liquor cabinet downstairs; and, she recalls, she has some prescription painkillers left over from having her wisdom teeth out last year...

You can see from Carly's story that, as she starts to fight the reality, she not only experiences pain (hurt and anger), which anyone would feel in a situation like this, but she also starts to suffer. In other words, she's not just feeling the initial hurt and anger, but as she fights the situation, these emotions intensify, and others—like resentment, bitterness, and fear—join in. The pain is inevitable; the suffering is optional. The suffering is what makes it more difficult to bear, and what often ends up leading to unhealthy choices.

Can you relate to Carly's experience? Are you able to recognize the times in your life when not accepting a painful situation has led to you suffering? Think about a situation that is happening for you now, or has happened fairly recently. It doesn't have to be a great big situation. These kinds of situations can arise on a smaller scale on a daily basis; for example, a fight you have with a friend, a hurtful comment someone makes, or a grade that disappointed you. Remembering that pain is unavoidable, think about how you experienced the "pain" of this situation, and then think about how you experienced the "suffering" of this situation. It might help to think about it like this: Your first reaction to the situation is usually the pain (remember primary emotions from chapter 5). You have a fight with your friend and you feel angry at her; you feel hurt at the hurtful comment; or you feel disappointed at the grade you got. The suffering tends to come when you've had more time to think about (judge!) the situation. You have a fight with your friend and you start to judge her, so now you feel not only the initial anger but also resentment and bitterness; you judge the person who was hurtful to you, so now you feel not only hurt but also angry; or you judge yourself for the grade you got, so now you feel not only disappointed but also ashamed.

Once you've gotten the idea of pain versus suffering, think about what suffering looks like for you. What actions do you take to make yourself feel better when it seems as though you can no longer tolerate the suffering? For many people, suffering leads to unhealthy actions, much like what Carly was beginning to consider, perhaps turning to drugs or alcohol to numb themselves. Some people vent their feelings by throwing temper tantrums; other people turn to self-harming behaviors or suicide attempts. Still others get stuck in self-pity and stop trying to improve their situation.

Take a few moments to think about what your experience of suffering is typically like: do you engage in behaviors that make things better for you, or do you do things that worsen the situation?

Reality Acceptance

You already have a hard time managing your emotions, so what can you do differently that will help you reduce your suffering and experience only the pain that is inevitable in any human life? You can stop fighting your reality and start practicing the skill of *reality acceptance*.

What Does Accepting Reality Mean?

First and foremost, accepting something does *not* mean that you approve of it, that you are okay with it, or that you don't want things to change; rather, it just means that you are acknowledging reality as it is. Acceptance means that you stop trying to deny your reality. It's putting a stop to the judgments about the situation, and instead acknowledging what is. It's taking out the "shoulds" and no longer spending so much energy wishing things were different.

To help you see how this works, I want you to take some time to think about a situation you were able to get to acceptance with—something that was painful for you, that you likely started out fighting, but that at some point were able to acknowledge as your reality. Examples might be the death of someone you cared about, the loss of a relationship, or not getting something you really wanted. Now think about what it was like for you once you got to acceptance with that situation. What was different for you? How did you feel once you were able to accept it?

Most people say that they felt "lighter," "relieved," or "like a weight had been lifted." Usually you'll find that, when you get to acceptance, the situation loses the power it had over you—you don't think about it as often as you once did, and when it does come up for you, the emotions that arise within you are much less intense than they used to be. It's not as consuming. There's less anger and fewer anger-related emotions associated with it.

Remember that this skill, like all the other DBT skills, will not make the pain go away, but it will make your suffering dissipate and, over time, disappear. And when you can reduce the emotional load you're carrying with you all the time, you'll be better able to manage the emotions that come up when difficult situations arise on a daily basis.

To go back to Carly's example, accepting the reality that Roy is no longer her friend isn't going to take her pain away, of course. She'll feel grief and sadness for her loss for some time, and she'll feel hurt and angry if he continues to treat her disrespectfully. What acceptance will take away, though, is her suffering: her anger, bitterness, and resentment. Over time, Carly will find that she thinks about the situation with Roy less often, and when she does think about it, it'll hurt less. She'll probably also find that she'll be more able to move on, letting go of that relationship, and finding other, healthier friendships.

So, you're probably wondering by now, how do you get to acceptance? Following is an exercise to help you practice this skill. Of course, mindfulness is the important first step toward accepting reality, since you have to be aware of the reality-fighting thoughts as they arise before you can start to reach for acceptance.

Exercise: Accepting Reality As It Is

Begin by focusing on your breath, just observing the physical sensations of breathing. When you're ready, allow yourself to become aware of what arises within you and to sense what is asking for acceptance. You'll know what is asking for acceptance because it will be something that continues to repeat itself, like a theme. For example, notice if your thoughts continue to return to a specific situation or person, or if a certain emotion repeatedly arises within you. When these themes emerge, you'll recognize that these are the things that are asking to be accepted. These themes remain because, on some level, we continue to resist them—we might feel a fear or aversion toward them, or perhaps we're judging the experience, trying to push it away or ignore it.

So notice the experience—the thoughts, the emotions—and then allow yourself to notice the feeling about the experience, perhaps an urge to push it away, a discomfort around having the experience, and so on. Just allow yourself to become aware of it.

As you notice these themes you're stuck in, and to help you begin to let go of them, acknowledge what is present and consider these questions: what is your experience? Do you want it to change? Is there a difficult emotion, thought, sensation, or other experience that you're refusing or denying in some way, or that you want to be over or to go away?

Practicing Reality Acceptance

Once you've identified what needs to be accepted, you can start practicing the four steps to reality acceptance.

1.   Make the choice.

     First, think of a situation you know you're fighting. The next thing you need to do is *choose* whether or not acceptance is something you want to work on with this situation. I've done my best to convince you that this skill will be helpful for you, but you're the one who has to be willing to try it, or it just won't work.

2. Make the commitment.

   If you decide to work on this skill, the next step is making a commitment to yourself to practice acceptance with that situation from this point forward. With the commitment, however, you're not done—just because you've committed doesn't mean it's going to come easily. But without the commitment, it's easier to fall back into old patterns. Committing means that this is a goal for you, and you're going to work hard to achieve it.

3. Notice the fighting.

   When you notice your thoughts have turned back in the direction of *It's not fair,* or *It shouldn't be this way,* just notice that this has happened. As best as you can, don't judge yourself; remember that it's natural for your thoughts to turn back in this direction, especially when you first start practicing acceptance. Like any skill, it will take time and practice.

4. Reach for acceptance.

   The final step, once you've noticed those reality-fighting thoughts come up, is to reach for acceptance again. Turn your mind away from fighting reality and toward acceptance. Remind yourself that you've committed to working on accepting, and think of the reasons it will be helpful for you.

I call these last two steps the "internal argument" that takes place within us. You'll notice that you're back to fighting reality: *It's not fair,* or *It shouldn't be this way;* and you then reach for acceptance with your mind: *It is what it is. I decided to work on accepting this situation because I don't want it to have this power over me anymore. I'm going to keep working on accepting this.* Of course, that's not the end of it; you'll start to fight again, maybe even right away: *But it's not fair that I have to put so much effort into this when it shouldn't have happened in the first place.* So again, when you notice those fighting thoughts, return to accepting: *But it did happen, and I know it's going to help me if I can stop fighting it…* and so on.

When you first begin practicing accepting reality, you might have to reach for acceptance many times in just one minute; that's okay, because you've already reduced your suffering in that minute by not letting yourself remain stuck in reality-fighting mode. And bit by bit, the time that you're accepting will increase to outweigh the time you're fighting. One of the keys here is being patient and, of course, practicing.

What Acceptance Isn't

People often have different understandings of what acceptance means, and this sometimes gets in the way of their ability to use this skill. Let's look at some of the things that tend to get in the way of people being open to the idea of acceptance.

Acceptance Doesn't Mean Approval

I know I already mentioned this, but it bears repeating: acceptance does not mean that you approve of the situation, that you like it, or that you want it to be the way it is. Many people have been through extremely difficult, emotional, and even traumatizing situations and events in their lives. For example, some people have survived wars, or been victims of crimes, or witnessed people doing terrible things to others, or been abused or neglected by the people who are supposed to care for them. The pain generated by these experiences is often worsened because people fight these realities, which creates suffering for them. In discussing acceptance with these kinds of situations, people will often say that the experience is not acceptable and that they shouldn't be expected to accept it.

If you're thinking this way, ask yourself, if you can't accept the reality, can you acknowledge that it *is* your reality? And really, how can you not acknowledge that this is your reality? This is what reality acceptance is about—not liking something or approving of it, but just acknowledging that it is.

Acceptance Doesn't Mean Forgiveness

Sometimes people believe they have to forgive the person who has caused them pain in order to move on. However, I see reality acceptance as an alternative to forgiveness, and my own opinion is that not everything is forgivable. To me, the idea of forgiveness is somewhat about the person doing the forgiving—it helps you let go and move on if you can forgive. But in my mind, forgiveness is also about the other person—there's an element of absolving him of responsibility, of saying "It's okay." But reality acceptance has nothing to do with the person who caused you pain—it's all about you, about reducing your suffering.

Here's an example to help you understand these points about reality acceptance.

136

✳ Casey's Story

Casey's best friend, Simon, had changed at the beginning of ninth grade. He became withdrawn, he barely ever invited Casey over to his house anymore, and he would often make excuses to not go out on the weekend. They were still good friends, and Casey knew there was something going on with Simon, but he couldn't figure out what it was, and Simon wouldn't talk about it. One day in gym class, the two were side by side in the locker room, and Casey caught sight of some bruises on Simon's chest and back. Simon realized that Casey had seen his injuries, and he quietly told Casey to leave it alone. Casey realized that his friend was being abused.

    His first response was disbelief: No way. I know his parents; they wouldn't do this. *And this soon turned to fighting reality, which increased his anger:* This is awful; it shouldn't be happening. Why wouldn't he tell me about this? I'm his best friend! *Once Casey was able to sort things through in his head, however, he was able to get to acceptance:* Okay. This is what's happening—Simon's father lost his job a few months ago; I know he's been frustrated. And evidently he's not dealing with it, and he's taking it out on Simon. Now what do I do about it?

So you see here that Casey isn't approving of the situation or saying it's okay that it's happening. He's just acknowledging that it *is* happening. Secondly, you see that Casey isn't forgiving Simon's father; he's not absolving him of responsibility or letting him off the hook for what he's done. He's acknowledging reality as it is.

Accepting reality is about deciding that you don't want to continue spending so much time and energy experiencing all these painful emotions about a situation—a decision that also reduces your suffering. It's about realizing that fighting reality isn't going to change your reality and that fighting reality is actually a waste of energy because it doesn't accomplish anything productive. Acceptance is what helps you let go and move forward.

Acceptance Doesn't Mean You Give Up

Some people get stuck with this skill because they think if they accept a situation, it means they're giving up on trying to change it. This is completely not the case—and if you really think about this skill, you'll see that acceptance, or acknowledging your reality as it is, means that you have to accept a situation before you can work toward changing it.

Think about what would have happened if Casey had continued to fight the reality of his best friend being physically abused by his father. If he had continued to say *It shouldn't be happening; it's not right,* he'd never get to the question *What can I do about it?* It's only by accepting reality as it is that we can figure out if there's something we can do to change that reality, and it's only by accepting reality that we free up the energy we were spending fighting reality to work to make those changes.

You Can Accept Only What Is Reality

Often people have difficulty with acceptance because they're trying to accept things that aren't actually reality—like the future. If something hasn't actually happened, it's not reality, and we therefore can't work on accepting it. An example of this is trying to accept that you're not going to get into the college you want. Many people will try to do this because they think they're being realistic, and it helps them prepare. But the reality is that we can't know what the future holds, and in fact, there are so many possible futures that if all you're doing is trying to accept all the possible futures in your life, you won't have time to do anything else! So if your average is 80 percent and the admission criteria for the school you want is 85 percent or over, you practice accepting that your average is 80 percent—*that's* the reality. Once you get your letter and it says "We're sorry"...well, that's the time to start practicing acceptance that you didn't get into the college you wanted, but not before then!

You might be thinking, however, that some things are inevitable. And yes, this is true: A few years ago, my grandmother was diagnosed with terminal cancer and given one month to live. I would sometimes find myself going into the future and imagining what it would be like when she passed away: how sad I would feel, the pain of seeing my mother grieving the loss of her mother, how much I would miss her, and so on. But in those times, even though I knew that her death was inevitable, I kept bringing myself back to the present, reminding myself that even though it was inevitable, it hadn't happened yet. And although it was inevitable, it wasn't going to be helpful for me to live her death over and over again before it even happened! So in this instance, you can ask yourself, *If this is inevitable, do I really want to live it repeatedly?* Doing so only causes you to go through the pain over and over again. (And by the way, my grandmother lived another five months, so here's one more example of how we can't know what the future holds!)

139

Judgments are another area where people get stuck with this skill. A judgment is a judgment; it's not a fact, and it's therefore not reality. So you can't accept that you're a loser, because that isn't reality. Instead, look at the realities that lead you to judge yourself as a loser: perhaps you didn't get into the college you wanted, maybe you don't have many friends, or maybe you didn't make the sports team you tried out for. In these instances, these are the realities you're working on: *I didn't get into the college I wanted*; *I don't have as many friends as I'd like*; and *I didn't make the team.*

Was That Really Acceptance?

Sometimes it's confusing because you think you've gotten to acceptance with something, but then something happens and here comes the suffering once again! If this happens, it doesn't mean that you weren't accepting. It simply means that you've been triggered back to non-acceptance. You might have had a difficult situation that you've been accepting of for years, but then something happens that causes you to (temporarily) go back to fighting that reality.

Let's say your parents split up when you were twelve. You're fifteen now, and you're over it. You've got the routine down pat—Monday and Wednesday and every other weekend you're with your dad. You spend time at the park, where he's been teaching you how to pitch so you can try out for the baseball team next year. One weekend, though, you get to his place and instead of going to the park to work on your pitching, he introduces you to his new girlfriend and her four-year-old son. How would you feel? What would your thoughts be about this situation?

I think most people would probably have some painful emotions around this: probably fear or anxiety, possibly sadness. And for some people, at least some of these emotions would result from reverting back to fighting the reality: *Why can't Mom and Dad just work things out? We'd all be happier if we were living together, and I wouldn't have to put up with his girlfriend and a loud kid in the house,* or *Mom and Dad never should've broken up in the first place; they're being stupid, and now Dad's moving on and life is going to suck even more.* The fighting and the judging increase your suffering and make the situation even more difficult for you to bear. But when this happens, remember it's normal, and you're not starting back at square one—you've gotten to acceptance with this situation before, and now you know the steps you can take to help you get back there again.

What Do You Need to Accept?

You've probably gotten the point that all the DBT skills you've learned so far aren't skills that you can practice for a while until things get better, and then you move on and leave them behind. These skills are about changing the way you live your life, and the way you think, so that you'll live a happier, healthier life in the long run. But making changes like this doesn't happen overnight. Think about all the time you've spent fighting all the realities that have been painful in your life so far. You can't just decide you're going to change it and have it happen quickly— unfortunately! In fact, sometimes once people learn about this skill, they have a hard time accepting that they've played a part in maintaining their own suffering for so long because they've been caught up in fighting their reality—in other words, they have a hard time accepting their non-acceptance!

So let's talk about how you can effectively practice this skill—first, by acknowledging (if this is the case for you) that you have contributed to your own suffering by fighting reality. Again, welcome to the human race! It is what it is; you didn't even know about this skill until an hour ago!

Next, it can be helpful for you to really think about what the realities are in your life that you need to accept: your past non-acceptance, perhaps? Or your parents' divorce, the death of a pet or grandparent, or maybe a disability that prevents you from doing certain things? Sit down with a pen and piece of paper, and make a list of the things in your life that you need to accept.

Once you've made your list (and you might find you need to add to it later on, but don't worry; once you start practicing you'll also find you can remove situations now and then!) I suggest that you start off by practicing with situations that are somewhat less painful for you. That way, you'll be more likely to get to acceptance sooner (since the more painful something is, the more difficult it is to accept and the longer it will therefore take), and you'll learn that you really can do this, and that it really does reduce your suffering. By starting with the less painful situations, you'll increase your self-confidence so that you can gradually work your way up to the more painful situations in your life that you would like to accept. Here are some suggestions for situations you could start practicing with on a daily basis:

* The next time you get a grade that you're not happy with, don't fight it by thinking about how you should have done better, or that the teacher has it in

for you; instead, tell yourself, *It is what it is* (and then maybe talk to the teacher about why she gave you this grade, and how you might do better on the next assignment).

* When you find your sister using the computer when you really need it, rather than getting worked up about how she's always making your life more difficult, practice reality acceptance (and perhaps say something to her if you need the computer for a school assignment).

* When you find yourself standing at the end of the line in the cafeteria, rather than allowing yourself to get angry about how many minutes of your lunch hour are ticking by, accept it. (And tomorrow you can bring your lunch!)

* When you have to change your plans because it's raining outside and going to the beach is clearly out, practice reality acceptance.

Again, take some time to make your own list of situations, past or present, that are continuing to cause you suffering and that you want to work on accepting. Remember as you do this to stick with realities—don't go into the future, and stay away from judgments. It can also help to be specific about the situations you're writing down. Instead of trying to accept that you've "made poor choices," be clear about what the choices are that you regret; for example, maybe it's hard for you to accept that you remained friends with someone who didn't treat you well.

Your Next Steps

So here's another skill that will help reduce the emotional pain in your life, which in the long run will help you survive the emotional roller coaster you've been riding. It may have occurred to you, of course, that acceptance is something that comes naturally to an extent—you may have many examples of painful situations that have happened in your life that you've come to accept, without consciously thinking about or practicing this as a skill. It's true that, as time passes and we move forward, most things tend to become less painful. But think about how helpful it will be now that you can consciously work on bringing acceptance to the painful situations in your life, and by doing so you'll get to acceptance and reduce your pain more quickly.

Your next steps, then, are to think about what situations in your life you need to practice acceptance with, as we discussed earlier. Remember that these are skills you need to bring with you, so continue to practice your other skills as well. If you haven't already, over time you will notice you're more able to manage the emotions. But don't forget to cut yourself some slack—these skills take time and practice, and you're working on undoing a lifetime of learning!

Chapter 8

Surviving a Crisis Without Making It Worse

Everyone has times in their lives when they find themselves dealing with strong emotions that make it more difficult to cope; for example, when someone you love dies or you otherwise lose a relationship with someone you care about, when you're moving and have to change schools and make new friends, or when you lose your job. Sometimes when this happens, you might experience urges to do things that you think will help you deal with these intense emotions in the short term, but that have some long-term negative consequences.

Until now we've been looking at skills that will help reduce the intensity of emotions—in other words, that help slow the roller coaster down a little. In this chapter, we're going to look at some skills that will help you cope in healthier ways when emotions are really intense, so that you'll be able to get through a crisis situation without making things worse for yourself.

What Is a Crisis?

In order to effectively use these skills, it will be helpful for you to first have a definition of what I mean by *crisis*. For our purpose, a crisis is an event or situation over which you have little or no control, or a problem that you can't solve (at least not right away), and which is causing you emotional pain. One example might be when you have a fight with your best friend. You're feeling angry with her and you're hurt; you might also be feeling anxious about the possibility of the friendship being over. But it's midnight, and you'll get into trouble with her parents if you try to call this late, so this isn't a problem you can solve right now. It's a crisis.

Or you've been working at a new part-time job for the summer. It's very physically demanding, and you've been having trouble keeping up with the workload. Your boss called you in for a meeting today and told you that it's not working out so you're being let go. This is a situation where you have no control—your boss has already told you there's no changing her mind, that you're just not able to keep up with the physical demands of the job—so there's nothing more you can do to change the situation. Maybe, to make things worse, you were counting on this income to help pay for your college tuition in the fall, and now you're going to have to apply for a student loan. This is a crisis.

Keep in mind that, as you may have noticed from these examples, a crisis will be different for different people—just because someone else doesn't understand why a situation is a crisis for you doesn't mean it's not a crisis!

Sometimes in a crisis, there are things you can do to change the situation or solve the problem so that your pain will be less intense—if this is the case, do them. If it's a time when you can call your best friend to try to resolve the argument you had, for example, do it! If you can solve the problem (and sometimes even if you're just taking steps toward solving the problem), you'll no longer be in crisis. Unfortunately, however, you'll often find that you have no control in the situation, or you might have some control but there's nothing you can do to try to solve the problem right now, and that's when your focus has to move to surviving the crisis without making things worse for yourself.

Before we get you looking at yourself, let's look at two examples of how people experience crisis situations in their lives, and the behaviors they engage in that often end up making things worse.

✳ Carmen's Story

Carmen's parents recently told him that they're separating. His dad is moving to another state for a new job, and Carmen will be living with his mom. Carmen was devastated, not only about the separation but also about his dad leaving; his dad has always been his best friend. He tried to talk to his father and asked to go with him, but his dad told him that it's out of the question, because he'll be traveling a lot for his new job, and he wouldn't be home enough to take good care of Carmen. His dad is planning to come visit once a month or so, and he wants Carmen to visit him at his new home on holidays.

When he first heard the news, Carmen had been stunned. Then he'd convinced himself that things would work out: his dad would let Carmen come stay with him, and life would still be tolerable. *But once even that hope was dashed, Carmen was beside himself with anger at his parents for not caring about how this would affect him, frustration at his father for not allowing him to come with him, and sadness and grief for what he saw as the inevitable loss of his relationship with his dad.*

Carmen's emotions were really intense, and he didn't know what to do with them. He started lashing out at his parents regularly—sometimes it made him feel a tiny bit better (and sometimes more than a tiny bit!) to make them hurt too. He also started staying out past his curfew, another way of making them suffer because he knew they worried about him. When his parents grounded him, that was fine—he would just avoid them, staying in his room playing video games all day so he didn't have to think about things. Unfortunately, this wasn't actually helping Carmen deal with things, and in fact was making things worse for him and his relationship with his parents in the long run.

✳ Stephanie's Story

Stephanie was eighteen when she started her first year at college. She had been so excited—a new school with new people, taking courses she was actually interested in, and working toward a career in business. After a few weeks, though, the new environment and the stress of being away from her family for the first time began to take a toll. Stephanie's stress skyrocketed as she tried to get everything done for her classes and also get involved with social clubs and activities at school. She began missing classes because she was so tired in the mornings, which increased her anxiety as she started worrying about her grades. Soon Stephanie felt as though she was spiraling out of control—she was having panic attacks, missing home and feeling down, and falling behind in her classes.

Trying to cope with her plummeting mood and increasing anxiety, Stephanie started smoking marijuana. She had smoked a bit in high school and recalled the feeling of calmness it would often bring on, and she thought it might help her feel better. It did help with her anxiety in the short term, but in the long run, Stephanie ended up further and further behind in her classes, and this brought her mood down even more.

Do you have a crisis going on in your own life right now? If you do, what are you doing to get yourself through it? If you can't think of something in the present that you would define as a crisis (lucky you!), think about some situations you've dealt with in your past that might fit the bill, just to make sure you get what we're talking about here. What's an example of a crisis for you?

What to Do in a Crisis

We've just looked at two teens in crisis who aren't coping in healthy ways. In fact, the way Carmen and Stephanie are trying to cope with their problems is actually making those problems worse, because they're caught up in their emotional selves, and they're letting the emotional roller coaster run away with them as a result. When emotions get this intense, it's sometimes easy to let things just spin out of control—but of course, that's not

---

effective; it's not helping either of them work toward their long-term goals.

What Do You Do to Cope?

Before we look at skills that will help you cope in healthy ways, think for a moment about the things you currently do to try to get yourself through a crisis. When your emotions start to get intense, or you start to feel out of control, what do you do to try to get back on track?

Most people have at least a couple of things they turn to that aren't healthy. Stephanie turned to substance use; Carmen turned to lashing out and playing video-games. Other behaviors might be overeating for comfort or undereating as a way of feeling in control; sleeping to escape; spending money, gambling, or shoplifting; or even turning to self-harming behaviors (for example, cutting, burning, or hurting yourself in other ways) or thoughts of suicide. If these last two apply to you at all, it's urgent that you ask someone you trust for help, whether it's your parents or another family member; your family doctor; a teacher, coach, or someone else you trust at school; a religious leader, and so on. When problems get this out of control, people often need help dealing with them, and asking for help is a sign of strength, not weakness.

Thinking About the Consequences

Looking at the negative consequences of your actions can often help stop you from falling back into these patterns in the future. Although this may sound obvious, you might be surprised at how often people just avoid thinking about this—which makes sense, because it's usually easier to keep acting the same way you always have, even if there are negative consequences. Making changes takes energy and effort!

If you're serious about surviving the emotional roller coaster, though, then this is a must: the behaviors people get stuck in when in crisis are often self-destructive, or at the very least end up feeding into emotional pain in the long run, in one way or another. Look at Carmen's story, for example. He's been lashing out at his parents, which might make him feel a little better in the short term. But over time, behaving the way Carmen has been will not only cause his relationships with his parents to suffer but will probably also lead to feelings of guilt and a loss of self-respect. And avoiding the situation by turning to gaming will likely make things worse in the long run as well. Do you recall from chapter 2 that when you try to suppress or ignore emotions they don't go away, and in fact they often get stronger?

So the first thing you need to do is think about what you do when you're in a crisis, and figure out which of these behaviors often (or always) come with negative consequences. In other words, which of your behaviors are actually making the situation worse for you? And don't worry—at this point, I'm not going to ask you to try to change that behavior. Remember, step one is always about increasing your awareness, so for right now, thinking from your wise self, take an honest look at the things you do when you're in crisis, and write down the things that might be making the situation worse.

In DBT, we do a pros and cons chart to help us look at the positive and negative consequences of certain behaviors. The

DBT version may be a little different from charts you've done before because it has four boxes instead of just two columns. So take a look at the example I've given using Carmen's behavior of lashing out at his parents, and read through the entries I've provided for each box to help you think about this.

Pros of Lashing Out at My Parents	Cons of Lashing Out at My Parents
• Makes me feel a little better to hurt them • Helps them see how hurt and angry I am • It pushes them away • It's easy	• I feel guilty later • They get angry with me • They don't want to spend time with me • I get grounded • It pushes them away
Pros of Using Skills Instead	**Cons of Using Skills Instead**
• I feel better about myself • My relationship with my parents is better • No guilt • I don't get into trouble • I learn to cope in other ways instead	• It's hard • I don't know what to do with my feelings instead • I have nowhere to put my anger • They might not understand how hard the separation is for me if I don't lash out at them

Your next step is to look at the list you made of behaviors that might be problems for you at times. If you have more than one behavior on your list that you can see has negative consequences in some ways, I want you to choose just one. Then, thinking about that one specific behavior, pull out a piece of paper and draw a chart like Carmen's, with two rows and two columns. In the top left box, write down any pros (benefits) you can think of to the behavior; how does doing this help you? In the top right box, write down what the cons (costs) are to the behavior: how does doing this harm you?

Then, in the bottom left box, write down the pros of using skills instead of engaging in the behavior: what are the positive consequences when you don't (or can't) do that behavior or activity? And finally, in the bottom right box, write down the cons of using skills instead of engaging in the behavior: what are the negatives of not engaging in that behavior? (You may have noticed that some consequences might be both positive and negative—and yes, that's okay!) While you're doing your own chart, as best as you can, don't censor yourself. If something pops into your mind, write it down, even if you think you've already said it. The point of this activity is to help you look at your behavior from a different perspective and see the bigger picture.

If you get stuck, you can also think about these questions: How do you feel about yourself when you do, or don't do, the behavior? Does the behavior have an effect on your relationships with friends and family? Does it affect your performance at school or in sports or other activities that are important to you? Is the behavior helping you move toward your long-term goals? (Remember, also, that you want to consider long-term as well as short-term consequences.)

If you've gotten this far, you've made a great start, but you're not done yet! We want to make sure you're filling this chart out while you're in your wise self. If you're in your emotional self, maybe even having the urge to do the behavior you're analyzing in your chart, chances are you'll come up with more benefits than costs. We want this to be as objective as possible in order to give you a better understanding of your behavior, so it's a good idea to come back to the chart a few times over the next week or so. When you read it with fresh eyes, you might find you want to add some things or delete some. Make some changes; just do your best to do so from your wise self.

If you'd like, once you've completed your chart, you can also add an extra step: rather than just looking at how many statements you have in each column, you may find it more effective to grade each statement. For example, for Carmen, the pro of making his parents see how much he hurts might be important, but it might not be as important to him as the con of his parents not wanting to spend time with him anymore. So Carmen might find it helpful to give each statement a number, say from 0 to 5, so that he can see how important each one is to him; he can then add up each column so he ends up with a numeric value for each, which might give him a more objective perspective than just seeing statements in the various columns.

Whichever way you choose to do your chart, ideally you'll have done it over time from your wise self. And usually, if this is the case, you'll see that the behavior is one that would be effective for you to change. Remember, though, that just because you're setting it as a goal for yourself doesn't mean you can expect it to change right away. This is just increasing your awareness—the first step. Now let's take a look at what will come next, if you decide you want to work on this as a goal.

Using What's Worked Before

The good news is that, even if you fall back into these unhealthy ways of coping at times (or frequently!), you probably also act in healthier ways at times as well. Take a moment to think about ways you cope sometimes that don't have those negative consequences attached. When you're having a crisis—a problem that can't be solved and that's causing you pain—what are some things you do to get your mind off it? For example, you might get together with a friend, or call someone to talk; maybe you try to cheer yourself up by watching your favorite TV show or listening to music that makes you feel good.

Distracting Yourself from the Crisis

In this section and the next, we're going to focus on ways you can get through a crisis without making things worse for yourself; first, by distracting yourself from the problem. Often, when you're in a crisis, it can be really tough to get your mind off the situation. You know there's nothing you can do (or you've already done everything you can), but your brain just keeps going back there. You dwell on it, you rehash it, and this just keeps you stuck in those painful emotions.

Distracting yourself is about getting your mind off the crisis and focusing (as best as you can, mindfully) on something else. In other words, you start an activity, and you keep bringing your mind back to that activity over and over again, accepting (over and over again) when your mind keeps wandering back to the painful situation. One important thing to remember about these skills is that they're not going to solve the crisis, or

155

make the problem or your emotions go away; they will, however, help you *survive* the crisis (and the pain) without making things worse for yourself.

So how would you do this? Well, remember that you probably already do this sometimes, so first think about what activities you use to distract yourself. Next, take a look at the following list of activities you could use to distract yourself. As you're reading through this list, pull out a piece of paper and a pen (or your tablet, phone, or laptop!), and make your own list.

Draw.

Talk to someone (about something other than your crisis!).

Go for a walk or hike.

Ride your bike.

Go skateboarding.

Look at pleasant photographs.

Do a word search or crossword puzzle.

Eat your favorite snack.

Write a poem.

Go rollerblading.

Play solitaire.

Finish something you started.

Go fishing.

Clean your room.

Meet up with a friend.

Think of times when you felt happy.

Give yourself a facial.

Teach your dog or cat a new trick.

Shovel snow.

Think about what you'd like to do when you're older.

Doodle.

Sing.

Go to a religious service.

Play cards.

Look at old yearbooks.

Buy yourself something nice.

Imagine your life after school.

Go to a movie.

Lie in the sun.

Go somewhere you can watch nature.

Burn some incense.

Tell someone you love them.

List the things you like about yourself.

Go bowling.

Get dressed up to go out.

Go somewhere you can feed the squirrels or birds.

Read the cartoons.

Look at the stars.

Upload some favorite photos on Facebook.

Go to a pet store and play with the animals.

Paint a picture.

Take a hot bath.

Play with your pet.

Watch your favorite TV show.

Play video games.

Play a board game with your sibling or a friend.

Bake some cookies.

Find a fun new ringtone for your cell.

Listen to a relaxation CD.

Surf the Internet.

Do arts and crafts.

Cook your family dinner.

Write a short story.

Daydream.

Watch a new TV show.

Buy someone a gift.

Take photographs of things you like.

Go to websites to read funny jokes.

Plan your summer vacation.

Laugh.

Pray.

Go somewhere to people watch.

Smile at someone.

Reach out to someone you miss.

Plan a fun day out on the weekend.

Read a comic book.

Make something out of play dough or clay.

Update your Facebook status.

Check your e-mail.

Do homework.

Listen to music.

Go to the beach.

Knit or crochet.

Give yourself a manicure or pedicure.

Cut the grass.

Go for a picnic.

Go to the zoo or a museum.

Invite a friend over.

Download some iTunes.

Experiment with different hairstyles.

Send someone a card for no reason.

Give someone a compliment.

Walk barefoot in the grass or sand.

Close your eyes and imagine yourself in your favorite place.

Play a musical instrument.

Organize your room, or part of your room.

Dance.

Write someone a letter or e-mail.

Help someone.

Learn to do something new.

Go skiing or snowboarding.

Watch a movie.

Scrapbook.

Journal.

Play a sport you enjoy.

Do something nice for your family or a friend.

Light some candles.

Rearrange your bedroom.

Do something to please your parents.

Explore a new area in your neighborhood.

Take a nap.

Play Wii.

Go to the mall.

Go somewhere you'll be around other people, like a park.

Go for a jog.

Do a sudoku puzzle.

Go swimming.

Fly a kite.

Watch funny videos on YouTube.

Of course, this list isn't exhaustive, but you'll probably find some ideas here of activities you could do that might get your mind off your crisis for a little while and that won't have the same negative consequences as some of the activities you might normally do. And, the good news is, we're not done yet! Before you move on, though, make sure you've started your own list of distracting skills, and keep it handy so you can add to it.

The idea of making your own list is that, when your emotions get intense and start to take over, it's usually really difficult to think about what you can do in that moment to help yourself. If you have a list of activities, you don't have to think—you just pull out your list and do the first thing on it. If you find that the first activity isn't really distracting you, or you're not able to focus on it very well, then you move to the next thing on your list, and so on, so make sure your list is as long as you can possibly make it! And keep it handy—put it on your phone or tablet, make some photocopies and keep one in your desk drawer or night table, keep one in your backpack or locker—so that you can pull it out when a crisis strikes.

Right now, though, make sure you keep it with you so you can keep writing as we look at the next set of skills, which will help you soothe yourself.

Soothing Yourself

For this set of skills, you're basically going to think about your five senses and what you find soothing to your senses. In other words, what can you do that might help you feel a little calmer, more relaxed, or more at peace? Just like the distracting skills, these skills aren't going to solve the problem for you; remember, the goal is to prevent yourself from falling into the problematic behaviors that often make things worse for you. So take a look at the examples below, and be sure to add things to your list as you get some ideas. You may find that some of the ideas here already came up in the distracting section, and that's okay. Remember, the idea is to brainstorm because you want your list to be as long as possible, so don't worry about a little repetition.

✳ Smell

What is soothing to your sense of smell? Some people enjoy the smell of flowers, incense, or perfume. You could light scented candles or buy some aromatherapy oils. Sometimes people enjoy the smell of baking or cooking.

✳ Sight

What do you enjoy looking at? Photographs of people, pets, or other things you really care about can be soothing. Or you might be someone who loves to look at nature—where can you go to do this? Your backyard, or a nearby park? I have one client who loves to sit in front of her fish tank and feels soothed just by watching her fish.

✳ Hearing

An obvious one here is music; is there a certain type of music you find soothing? Many people find nature sounds soothing. And what about the sound of someone's voice? You may find that just hearing your parents' voices, or the voice of a friend, can be soothing.

✳ Touch

Is there anyone nearby who can give you a hug, if that would be soothing for you? How about a pet who might enjoy being petted as much as you might enjoy the soothing sensation of petting? Putting a hot water bottle on your neck, your feet, or somewhere else that's comforting for you is another way of soothing yourself through touch.

❋ Taste

Do you have a favorite snack you can indulge in? Some people enjoy the taste of herbal tea or a candy to suck on. You'll notice, however, that I've left this sense until last. That's because some people overindulge already by soothing themselves through taste, and this can become unhealthy and have negative consequences. If eating is a problem in some way for you, you might still use the herbal tea or sucking candy idea; if even that is too difficult or might trigger other urges for you, then stick to your other senses. If this isn't a problem, however, you can soothe yourself through taste as long as it doesn't become your regular way of self-soothing.

Practicing mindfulness meditation, guided imagery, or relaxation exercises can also be soothing, so if you have something like this that you do already, add it to your list. If you haven't had much experience with these practices yet, hopefully you're getting the idea of mindfulness practice and can find some specific practices that are soothing for you. You can also google mindfulness meditations and relaxation exercises, and try some out to see if you find any that resonate for you.

You may have noticed in learning about these self-soothing skills that many of these activities are also a good way of taking care of yourself on a regular basis, so that you'll actually find yourself in crisis less often. This is because, when you're taking the time to do activities like these that are calming, relaxing, and soothing for you, you'll be more able to handle stress and difficult situations, so they'll be less likely to turn into crises. So add these activities to your list to help you when you're in a crisis, and also think about what you might be able to do to take better care of yourself in this way on a more regular basis.

Dealing with Distressing Thoughts

When it comes to distressing thoughts (for example, when you're in a crisis and you can't get your mind off the problem, or you're having an urge to do something you know you'll regret later), our tendency as humans is to want to get rid of or stop these thoughts. It's often frustrating for people to learn that we really don't have control over the negative thoughts that pop into our heads; but, of course, we can control what we do about those thoughts.

The key to stopping the unwelcome thoughts, though, is actually to stop trying to get rid of them! The more you try to push thoughts away, the stronger and more intrusive those thoughts will become. Part of the problem with trying to get rid of thoughts is that, when we try not to think about something, our brain has to think about what it's not supposed to think about in order to try to not think about it. Don't worry if I've lost you—just try this exercise.

For the next thirty seconds, do your best to not think about pink elephants. Try as hard as you can to avoid thinking about gigantic pink elephants. Close your eyes if this makes it easier for you, but do your best to not picture their big, floppy ears; their thick, wrinkly trunks; and their long, thin tails. Stop thinking about them.

What did you notice? Most people notice that it's pretty difficult, if not impossible, to not think about pink elephants, because trying to suppress thoughts actually tends to trigger an increase in those thoughts. If you found that you were successful in not thinking about pink elephants, I promise you that if you continued to do the exercise, those thoughts would eventually intrude—it's just how our brains work.

Using Mindfulness to Let Go of Thoughts

The trick to getting rid of a thought you don't want is to be mindful of the thought. Don't judge it, but accept it; just acknowledge it or observe it, and you'll find that this helps reduce the strength of the thought. It will go away. Of course, it might come right back again! But mindfulness helps you change your relationship to your experience: rather than being afraid of or angry about thoughts that arrive and what they mean about you as a person, you accept them, and by doing so, you take away their power. Of course, mindfulness is often hard to use at the best of times, so turning to this skill when you're in a crisis is extra, extra hard! That doesn't mean it's not doable; it just means it takes a lot of practice and perseverance. To help with this, practice the following mindfulness exercise.

Exercise: Mindfulness to This One Moment

When in a crisis situation, being mindful to just this one moment can be especially helpful. There are no special instructions for this mindfulness practice—it's just about being mindful to whatever it is that you're doing in this one moment. In other words, if you're doing your homework, you focus on just doing your homework, with your full attention, and with acceptance of whatever your experience is in that moment. If you're walking your dog, focus on just walking your dog, bringing your attention back to the walk and your dog again and again, as best as you can, not judging yourself for wandering, and not judging yourself for the painful thoughts and emotions that might be coming up.

By focusing on what you're doing in this one moment, you can turn your attention away from the crisis and the distressing thoughts and emotions that are being triggered for you. Doing one thing at a time in the present moment, with your full attention and with acceptance, also helps you feel less overwhelmed in times of crisis. Just remember that skills are especially difficult to practice in stressful times, and as best as you can, don't judge yourself when you find your attention constantly wandering back to the crisis.

Of course, mindfulness is only one skill to help with distressing thoughts; let's turn now to look at some other ways of helping yourself with these thoughts when you're in a crisis.

Reframing

This skill focuses more on the way you think about a crisis. Again, it's not going to change the problem, but changing the way you're thinking about a problem can often help you not act on urges that might be coming up for you, urges that might make things worse for you in the long run. Following are some ways you can work on *reframing*, or changing how you're thinking about the crisis.

Encourage Yourself

Often, when we're thinking about a problem, we *catastroph-ize*: we think about the worst possible thing that could happen. If you recall Carmen's situation, for example, he was catastrophizing about his relationship with his father, assuming that since his parents were splitting up and his father was moving, their relationship was going to essentially end. Although it's a pretty typical human thing to think like this, you can probably see that it's really not helpful!

So one way of reframing is to counter this kind of thinking; when you notice you're catastrophizing, try to do something different. Mindfulness, of course, will be helpful—come back to the present and focus on the here and now. But in the here and now your problem still exists, so try to be more encouraging toward yourself instead of working on convincing yourself that things will be awful. Carmen could try saying something like *It's going to be really hard, and I don't like that this is happening, but I will get through it.* I want to point out here that I'm not telling you to think positive. It isn't going to be realistic for Carmen to just tell himself, *It'll be okay; it'll all work out*—his parents are splitting up, his dad is moving far away, and his life is about to change drastically. Not only will Carmen likely not believe these thoughts, they're basically invalidating his emotions, not acknowledging how angry and hurt he feels, which might actually end up making him feel worse. The idea, instead, is to stick to neutral thoughts.

It can also help if you try to think about what your best friend, parent, little sister, or someone else you know who really cares about you would say to you to reassure you and help you through this situation. Or, on the flip side, think of someone you really care about, and consider what you would say to her if she were going through this situation. We can't always be gentle and kind to ourselves when we need it, but we can sometimes get there if we can think about it from one of these different perspectives.

Compare

Another way of changing your thoughts through reframing is by comparing yourself to someone else who isn't doing as well as you are—in other words, recognizing that even though you're struggling right now, it could also be worse. For example, to recall Stephanie's situation, she could use comparing to reframe her thoughts: *I'm really struggling right now, and I don't like that I've turned to smoking marijuana to cope. But Charmaine had to drop out of school, so things could be worse.* It's really important to recognize that this skill has nothing to do with putting Charmaine down—rather, it's about helping you see the bigger picture and acknowledging that, although things are tough, they could also be worse. And, of course, we wouldn't want Stephanie to stop there—she also needs to keep working to make changes so that she doesn't end up dropping out of school too.

This is just one way of comparing, though—there are other ways of using this skill. Can you compare yourself now to a different time in your life when you weren't coping as well? If Stephanie had a history of substance abuse, for example, she might be able to tell herself, *Even though I'm struggling with my marijuana use, I haven't gone back to drinking like I did last year when things got really hard.*

You can also broaden the focus of this skill to a more global level. I've actually had to stop watching the news over the last few months of writing this book, because I was finding all the current crises in the world too distressing: disease, plane crashes, terrorism, and on and on. So how about this: *Yes, things suck in my life right now, but at least I'm not living under the threat of famine* (or war or drought or...take your pick). Hopefully you can see that this has nothing to do with minimizing anyone's pain or struggles; it's about helping you see things from a different perspective.

Putting These Skills Together

Here are the steps to follow to make it more likely you'll get through a crisis without doing things to make it worse.

1. Rate your urge.

    When you first notice an urge pop up, rate its intensity from 1 to 10 (where 1 means the urge is very slight, and 10 means the urge is really intense).

2. Set a timer for fifteen minutes.

    After rating your urge, try to put some time between noticing the urge and acting on it. The idea here isn't to tell yourself you'll never again give in to the urge—if this behavior has been with you for a while and has helped you cope, saying you're done with it will likely feel overwhelming and probably won't be effective for very long. Instead, commit to not acting on the urge for just fifteen minutes; for the next fifteen minutes, you'll act as skillfully as you can to prevent yourself from falling back into that old behavior. This will hopefully seem more doable, since you're not saying "forever," but you are putting some time between the urge and your action, giving yourself a chance to use skills instead of automatically acting on the urge.

Setting an alarm on your smartphone, tablet, or even a kitchen timer is really important—remember, the idea here is that, after you've rated your urge, you want to get your mind off the urge by using skills. It's really hard to get your mind off an urge when you keep checking your watch to see how much longer you have to wait!

3. Use your skills!

    While those fifteen minutes are ticking by, use the skills we've just gone through. Pull out your list of skills to distract and soothe yourself, and start working your way down it. Say, for example, that the first thing on the list of distracting activities you reviewed earlier is "Draw"; you would pull out your art supplies and start to draw. If that isn't distracting you from the problem, or if you're trying to draw and find you can't even concentrate enough to keep your mind on it, then you pack up your stuff and move on to the second thing on the list: talk to someone. So you call a friend and talk to her (remember, though— talk about something other than the problem!), and so on.

    If you've done a pros and cons chart on the behavior you're having an urge to do right now, you can also make a separate list of the cons of acting on the behavior, and the pros of using skills instead, and in times of crisis you can read this list to yourself to remind you of the reasons why you're trying to stop the behavior.

Again, this is something that's best done ahead of time, when you're not having the urge to do the behavior.

4. Rate your urge again.

    When your timer goes off, rate your urge again to see if it's come down in intensity. If it has, you can pat yourself on the back and go about your day. If it's stayed the same or is stronger, do your best to reset the timer, again making the commitment to not act on the urge for the next fifteen minutes, and go back to practicing skills.

Of course this is the ideal, but we live in the real world, and I'm well aware that sometimes it feels impossible to keep using skills and to not act on the urge. Sometimes you just give up and do the behavior, even when you know that it's making things worse for you. But here's the thing: even if you only set the timer once, and you don't act on the urge for fifteen minutes, you've just proven to yourself that you can use skills instead of acting on the urge. And hopefully the next time you'll be able to do it for thirty minutes, and then forty-five minutes, and so on.

Your Next Steps

I hope that, through reading this chapter, you've gained some insight about behaviors you've been using to try to get yourself through crisis situations but that have actually been making things worse for you in the long run. Of course, you may not have behaviors like this, and if you've come to the realization that you actually cope pretty well, that's one thing you won't need to work on changing in order to survive this emotional roller coaster you've been on. If you do have some behaviors that you need to look at changing, then first off, good for you for acknowledging this; and secondly, I hope you can muster up the courage to start working to change these. Change isn't usually easy.

If you've made the commitment to start working on at least one of these behaviors, though, pat yourself on the back—and now get to work! Make sure you're working on your list of distracting and self-soothing skills to help you not act on the urge when it arises. Keep practicing your mindfulness exercises to help you increase awareness of thoughts and emotions and to learn to tolerate these when they're distressing. And, of course, now you also have some ideas about how to change your thoughts when you recognize that you're catastrophizing or thinking about a crisis in other ways that are making it more difficult for you to tolerate.

I know it's a lot of work, so make sure you take it slowly and steadily. If you find yourself becoming overwhelmed, take a break and come back to it later. Remind yourself that you've been stuck on this ride for quite some time, and change doesn't happen overnight—but it certainly won't happen at all if you don't keep working at it. The good news is that, in the next chapter, we're actually going to focus more on the positives! So hang in there, and when you're ready, move on to chapter 9.

Chapter 9

The Building Blocks for Positive Emotions

Throughout this book you've been learning skills that will help you manage painful emotions and prevent extra emotional pain from arising. Hopefully you're using these skills and seeing results (even if they're only tiny ones right now), but unfortunately your mood isn't likely to improve without even more effort than you've been putting in already. I know—feeling better is hard work! But if you're regularly feeling down or depressed; if you're frequently anxious, worried, or nervous; if you're feeling angry, irritated, or annoyed quite often; or if you have difficulties with your mood swinging from one of these states to the next, it's going to take some additional work (and skills) for your mood to improve—and for you to have more ability to at least slow down this emotional roller coaster you've been riding. So that's what this chapter is about: what you can do to smooth out the roller coaster ride by increasing the pleasant emotions in your life.

Improving Your Mood Takes Work

Often when you're in emotional pain—for example, feeling depressed, anxious, or angry—you don't have the desire or drive to do certain things, even if you realize they might help you feel better. Unfortunately, while this is understandable and not unusual, it feeds into a vicious cycle: When you're not regularly doing activities that are enjoyable, relaxing, calming, soothing, or positive in some other way, your mood isn't likely to improve. Not only will you be less likely to experience pleasant emotions, but it's also more probable that you'll start to feel bored and unfulfilled, which will actually feed into your emotional pain. So what do you do?

Seeing the Positives

Let's start by looking at the way you see things when you're not feeling emotionally well. The way you feel affects the way you see things. When you're feeling content or satisfied with your life, you're more able to see the positives in life; when you have more emotional pain in your life, your focus tends to be more on the negative. Of course, it's not that more "bad" things than usual are actually happening during this period; it's just that you notice them more because of your emotional pain. Likewise, this pain makes it more difficult for you to notice anything positive that happens.

One thing we know now about the human mind, which doesn't help matters any, is that it has a *negativity bias*, a tendency to notice the negative over the positive, regardless of mood. If you think back to prehistoric times, this actually makes a lot of sense. To survive, our ancestors had to focus on the negative things that happened in order to learn from them, avoid them, and even try to prevent them from happening again—assuming they survived the first time around! For example, if the leader of your prehistoric clan hated strawberries and loved raspberries, and you spent a number of hours collecting strawberries when you could have been collecting raspberries instead (not knowing the leader's preference), he might have become very angry with you. The consequences might have been that you didn't get to sleep near the fire that night and so you were very cold and didn't sleep well; and the next day when your clan was attacked by a lion you couldn't run as fast because you hadn't slept well the night before, so guess who was lunch? If you survived the lion attack, or if you were fortunate and the lion didn't attack that day, you'd be likely to remember the clan leader's negative reaction to you for bringing home the strawberries!

So, historically, the negativity bias makes sense. But what does this mean for us now? Of course, in some ways, it still serves the same function of keeping us connected with the people in our lives who are important to us, although this doesn't usually have the same significance for survival that it used to, once we're self-sufficient. But by and large, it tends to create a lot of emotional pain, because we continue to focus on the negatives when we don't really need to. For example, if you have five interactions with your teacher during the course of your class today, and three are positive, one neutral, and one negative, which do you think will be the one on your mind when you're on your way home from school? Probably the negative and, of course, that negative focus will likely bring up some kind of emotional pain for you: perhaps frustration, shame, sadness, or anger. That's how our minds work.

Just because that's how our minds work, though, doesn't mean we can't change them! To do this, you need to purposely start noticing the positive things that are happening. Notice the small positives: the look on your dog's face when she greets you at the door, the stillness and silence on a winter's night as the snow falls in your backyard or as you sit on the deck under the stars, the pleasant smell of dinner cooking when you walk in the door, seeing someone smile at you as you pass each other on the sidewalk. These are events that would be likely to bring up pleasurable emotions for most people, but many of us miss out on those emotions because we're not paying attention. We're too busy focusing on the negatives instead—like the fact that your dog is jumping up on your clean pants, or the fact that it's snow-ing out and you'll have to walk to school in the snow tomorrow morning! The negativity bias is there, but you can retrain your mind to pay more attention to the positives. Make it your mission in life to start noticing some of those little positive events and to experience the pleasurable emotions that accompany them.

The following mindfulness exercise involves noticing when your focus has shifted to the negative, and using an analogy to help you change this.

Exercise: Mindfulness to Pleasant Experiences

Picture yourself going tobogganing. You carry your sled up to the top of the hill, place it in the snow, and slide down. At the bottom of the hill, you pick up your sled. You go back up to the top of the hill, place your sled in the same track in the snow, and slide down the hill. The more you do this, the deeper the track gets in the snow and the more easily the toboggan glides down the hill. In fact, if you try to move the toboggan over a little, you find that it quickly reverts back to that same track because it's become the path of least resistance.

Your mind is that toboggan, and that path is the negativity bias. Your mind is used to going down that same old path; it's easy, it's comfortable, and it doesn't take a lot of work. This mindfulness exercise is about starting to move your toboggan over. You need to start a new track down that hill; in other words, you need to get your mind to stop taking the path of least resistance (the negative) and work on developing a new, healthier path for the toboggan to go down—the path of positive thoughts. How do you do this?

First, notice when you're going down that same old path of negativity. Recognize it; don't judge it—just become aware of it. And then you can say to yourself, *I need to move my toboggan over*. If you can, find something positive in your present moment to focus on; for example, your cat snuggled up beside you, or the sun shining in through the window. Now *be with* that experience. Pay attention to it. Observe it. Allow the pleasurable emotions to sink into you. As with any mindfulness practice, your thoughts will likely wander; notice that, and bring them back to this moment and this positive experience.

Another way of doing this is to focus on a positive memory or image. One person I worked with, for example, had a wonderful memory of a positive interaction she had with someone she really cared about. When she noticed her toboggan going down that same old track in the snow, she would call on that memory and really focus on that pleasurable experience, recalling it in as much detail and feeling the emotions all over again.

That's how you move your toboggan over; you replace those negative thoughts with positive ones. Of course, like anything, it takes time and practice, but it's well worth the effort, and over time it will start to become more natural for you to go to the positive—you can turn your negativity bias into a positivity bias!

Of course, changing your mood isn't just about changing your thoughts. It's also about changing the way you live your life. Let's take a look now at other things you can start to do differently in your life to head in this direction.

Having Goals to Work Toward

Have you ever had a time in your life when you were kind of drifting along, not really knowing where you wanted to be going? You may not have had this experience yet, but trust me when I say it tends to be frustrating and confusing. Just having goals—both short-term and long-term—can help improve your mood. Knowing that you have a direction, and a purpose, even if it changes now and then, can help keep you grounded. So where are you at with goals in your life right now?

The activities for pleasurable emotions and to build mastery that we're about to look at can be short-term and long-term goals you're striving toward. It can also help if you think about your life in a more general sense: Where would you like to be one year from now? What about five years from now? Don't get me wrong; I don't think you have to have your entire life planned out! But it can be empowering to have at least a sense of where you'd like to be going, again, even if this changes from time to time. Having goals and direction in life helps you feel more fulfilled, and in turn helps with self-esteem.

Reaching a goal, of course, can often give you this as well. Hopefully, you'll not only enjoy doing what you set out to do but also have a sense of accomplishment, contentment, pride in yourself, and maybe even happiness, for getting there. And again, you'll probably also feel good about yourself, which will also improve your mood.

Pleasurable Activities

Remember what I said earlier about the fact that your mood often prevents you from doing things that might provide the opportunity for your mood to improve? Even though that's the case, you still have to push yourself to do these things. You might not feel like doing it, but if you don't do it, nothing is likely to change. So your first step is to think about activities, but don't aim too high: we're not looking for things that are going to make you "happy," and even the word "enjoyable" might be too strong. Instead, think along the lines of activities that might provide your mood with the opportunity to improve. Think contentment, relaxing, satisfying, peaceful. Think any kind of pleasurable emotion, no matter how small.

I find it's usually easiest for people to start with previous experiences, so think about what activities you already do, or used to do, that might fit the bill. It can help if you make a list of activities you do now that you sometimes find pleasurable, and activities you used to do. Think of things you might find pleasant; consider what activities your friends do that generate some interest or curiosity for you. If you're having a hard time thinking of enjoyable activities, grab a piece of paper and go through the following steps:

1. Write down any activities you can think of that might be pleasant, peaceful, relaxing, or interesting, or that might

generate some other pleasant emotion. For now, don't limit yourself. You're just brainstorming, so write down anything that pops into your head, even if it seems unrealistic for some reason.

2. If you're still having troubles thinking of activities, think about anything that's ever appealed to you as a possibility. Maybe you remember seeing a Facebook post about an underwater discovery or a TV show about astronomy, and it looked interesting to you—write it down. Maybe you have a friend who's recently discovered photography and you think it sounds cool—make a note of it. Don't worry right now about whether you can afford it, how you would get started, or whatever—just write it down!

3. If you're *still* having trouble thinking of activities, it's time for you to google. Search online for "fun things to do" or "interesting activities." You might be surprised to find that there are many online lists that might help you get started. You can also ask family and friends for suggestions.

4. Once you have your list, it's time to decide where you'd like to start. Pick whatever appeals to you the most (even if it's still not all that appealing!) and is doable to start with. If you don't have anything on your list that really seems doable, see how close you can get—you might not be able to go scuba diving in the Red Sea, for example, but you might be able to start taking scuba lessons, and you can probably join some online groups for scuba diving and underwater photography.

You may find that you often have things you'd like to do that aren't possible for some reason—you don't have the time, you aren't old enough, you can't afford it, and so on. But just because you can't do that exact thing doesn't mean there aren't ways to experience something similar; you just have to get creative sometimes! And keep in mind that the planning is often just as pleasurable as doing the activity itself. Even if you have to wait two years until you can afford your first diving trip, you can learn about it, plan it, fantasize about it, research it, and so on, and that can bring a lot of pleasant emotions as well.

You'll also want to have a variety of activities over time—some that are more involved and that you may need to work toward as longer-term goals, like scuba diving, and others that are simpler and available on a more regular basis, like reading, doing jigsaw puzzles, or learning how to cross-stitch. Remember that the more activities like these you have to turn to in your life, the more positive you will start to feel, and this, in turn, will make it easier for you to find pleasurable activities to pursue.

Building Mastery

While pleasurable activities are obviously important, you also need activities in your life that help you feel fulfilled, whether you enjoy doing them or not. This is the DBT skill of *building mastery*. Activities that build mastery help you feel productive and hopefully proud of yourself for having accomplished something, and so the list will look different from person to person. Building mastery isn't about the actual activity you're doing, but about the feeling the activity generates. For one person it could be getting his applications in for college, and for the next person it might be getting out of bed and making it to school on time. It could be raising your hand in class if you're usually a wallflower, or it might be auditioning for the school play. What matters is that the activity gives you a positive feeling about yourself and makes you want to say, "Hey, look what I did," even if the outcome isn't your ideal.

What do you do in your life already that gives you this feeling? What else could you be doing to achieve this sense of fulfillment more regularly?

Just Do It!

So here we are, back to that problem of your mood controlling your behavior—you're stuck in your emotional self. If there were one word I could remove from the dictionary, it would be "motivation." I hear so often from people that they "wish" they could do something or they "want" to do something, but they just don't have the motivation. People often get stuck in the trap of believing that they need to feel motivated before they can do something, when in fact as humans we often don't experience motivation until after we've started the activity we're trying to get motivated to do!

How often does this happen to you? Do you usually feel like doing your homework? How often are you motivated to get out of bed to go to school? Do you generally want to clean up your room on the weekend? And yet you (hopefully!) do these things anyway, because you know you have to do them, and because you know you're probably never going to really feel like doing them, so you don't wait for the motivation to come before you get started.

Quite often we don't feel like doing the things we have to do, and yet we do them anyway. So what's the difference between this and the things we just can't get ourselves to do? It seems to me that the difference is the thought that we *should* want to do certain activities. When it's something we know we never feel motivated to do, like homework, going to school, or cleaning up, it makes sense that we wouldn't want to do it. We do it anyway (although, granted, we may procrastinate!) because we know we're never really going to feel like doing it; we don't wait for the motivation to come.

But when it's something we think we should want to do—like activities we normally enjoy—we think we have to wait to want to do it. You *should* want to go to the movies with your friends, you *should* want to go to the baseball game with your dad, you *should* want to visit your cousins for the weekend. So when you find that you don't want to do it, you don't push yourself; you wait for the motivation to come. And that, of course, is not the effective thing to do; it's not acting from your wise self. Instead, when your mood is getting in the way of your doing things, you need to treat every activity like a chore: don't wait to feel like doing it—just do it! Scheduling activities into your day can also help you push yourself to do these things; the trick then is to make sure you treat it like an appointment and you follow through.

You might be surprised that once you've started doing the activity, you will actually feel like doing it, and you might even find that you enjoy yourself, even if it's just a bit.

Being Mindful of Your Emotions

The negativity bias that often prevents you from noticing the positives in your life when you're in a lot of emotional pain can also prevent you from feeling the pleasant emotions that arise. Sometimes this is because the feeling is short-lived; sometimes it's because the emotion isn't very strong—and let's face it, the pleasant emotions are often not nearly as strong as the painful ones! Either way, when you're on the emotional roller coaster, feeling depressed, anxious, or angry a lot of the time, it can be easy to miss out on those moments when a pleasant feeling comes up. But it's important to start training yourself to notice when this happens so you don't miss out on those positives.

Being mindful of your emotions, though, also involves being mindful of painful emotions. So not only do we not want you missing out on the pleasurable emotions when they come up but we also don't want you accidentally hanging on to the painful ones that come up. You may recall from previous chapters that when you're in emotional pain you tend to do things that keep the pain hanging on—like recalling other times you've felt this way, dwelling on the fact that this pain has already been going on for so long, and worrying about the pain never ending (chapter 1); judging yourself for the way you're feeling (chapter 4); and so on. So being mindful of your emotional pain means just that: being present with it and accepting of it, not doing things to try to get rid of it or escape it, but letting it dissipate on its own.

Here is a mindfulness practice to help you with this skill.

Exercise: Being Mindful of Your Emotions

Sitting in a comfortable position, begin by focusing on your breathing—not necessarily changing your breath, although if you have a breathing exercise that's comfortable for you, you can follow that specific practice. When you're feeling ready, draw your attention to whatever emotions are present for you right now, in this moment.

Remember that thoughts will likely come into your mind, and you might notice physical sensations or other distractions. Whatever comes into your awareness, just notice it: allow yourself to sense it, and label it without judging it. For example, you might notice that you have tension or pain in your· shoulders. As best as you can, don't judge the physical sensations, even if they're not what you would like them to be. Don't try to interpret the experience or think about what it might mean; just acknowledge it: *There is tension and pain in my shoulders.* You might notice that you're having judgmental thoughts about a situation in your life. Just notice this without judging it; for example, *I'm having judgmental thoughts about my friends at school.*

When you notice a feeling you're experiencing, do the same thing; without judging it, trying to push it away, or trying to change it in some way, just observe it and describe it to yourself; for example, *I'm feeling angry* or *I'm feeling bored.* It can also help if you repeat the name of the emotion to yourself three or four times; for example, *anxiety... anxiety...anxiety.*

In this way, you're acknowledging the emotion you're experiencing without trying to do anything about it. Remember that, when you can accept an emotion, it becomes less painful because you're not triggering any secondary emotions.

185

This exercise can also be helpful with the pleasant emotions you experience: by noticing that you're feeling and acknowledging it (for example, *contentment...contentment...contentment*), you can move away from the tendency to judge the emotion (as positive or negative), cling to the emotions you want to feel, or push away the emotions you don't like. Instead, you just allow yourself to experience whatever emotion is present in this moment.

Validating Your Emotions

The skill of self-validation from chapter 5 can help you be mindful of your emotions. Hopefully you recall how important it is to validate, or accept, your emotions instead of struggling against them or trying to get rid of or avoid them in some way. Validation also applies to pleasant emotions, in the sense that you don't want to try to cling to the emotion or try to make it stick around longer. If you've been feeling down, anxious, or angry a lot, it's understandable that you'd want a pleasant emotion like enjoyment or contentment to stick around as long as possible. The problem is that, as soon as you start thinking about how to make it stay, you're out of the present moment and thinking about the future, which essentially helps ensure that that pleasant emotion won't last long.

So as difficult as it is, stop struggling with the emotion that is there (either trying to make it go away or trying to keep it), and just allow yourself to experience it. If it's a painful emotion, it will gradually fade as you accept its presence and find ways to help yourself manage it. And if it's a pleasant feeling, it will stick around a bit longer while the positive experience is happening.

Your Next Steps

In this chapter we've changed our focus a bit from how to manage the painful emotions you're experiencing to how to increase the pleasurable emotions you'd like to experience more often. The bottom line is, there are lots of ways to do this, and it's important to be aware that your current emotional state will often get in the way of your doing the things that will generate the positives—if you let it. So even though you don't feel like doing the things that might improve your mood, you have to push yourself to do these things anyway. In other words, stop letting your emotional self control you, and listen to your inner wisdom!

There are lots of suggestions in this chapter, and it's up to you where you want to start. Whatever you do, make sure you continue to practice the skills you've already learned in this book. Remember, DBT skills are about making life changes, so don't expect to practice them for a while and then leave them behind. If you want things to get better and stay better, you have to continuously work to incorporate these skills into your life. This will take less energy as time goes on, and you'll find that the skills will start to come more naturally.

The good news is, you're almost at the end of this book. The bad news, perhaps, is that the last piece of work to be done is on relationships—and these, for sure, can make it more difficult to survive the emotional roller coaster. So when you're ready, let's head into the last chapter.

Chapter 10

Improving the Relationships in Your Life

While surviving the emotional roller coaster obviously has a lot to do with learning skills to help you manage your emotions in healthier ways, the relationships you have in your life (with family, friends, love interests, teachers, or coaches, among others) will also have an effect on your mood and on how well you're able to manage your emotions.

The people you surround yourself with have a large influence on how you feel, and how healthy and satisfying these relationships are will have an effect on not only your mood but on how you feel about yourself as well. So in this chapter we're going to take a closer look at relationships. You'll be asked to think about the relationships you currently have in your life and how satisfying and healthy they are, as well as whether you might need more people in your life in some way. You'll also learn some skills to help you ensure that your relationships will be healthier in the long run, which will go a long way toward helping you live an emotionally healthier life.

How Healthy Are You in Relationships?

Let's start by looking at what makes a relationship healthy. The defining word for me when it comes to relationships is "balance," which in my mind is almost synonymous with "healthy" for many things. But when we say we want our relationships to be balanced or healthy, what does that mean exactly?

* If you're healthy with relationships, you're going to have a variety of relationships in your life: a number of acquaintances, friends, and very close friends. There will be different people you know you can count on in different ways.

* If you're in a healthy relationship, it will be fairly balanced in terms of give and take. You can expect that you'll give to the other person at times, and at other times you'll be on the receiving end.

* In a healthy relationship, you can also expect that you'll be able to communicate openly with the other person. You'll be able to listen to your friend's concerns, and you'll also have the right to talk with her about things that are bothering you, and the two of you can work together to find solutions to problems that arise in your relationship.

* When you're healthy in your relationships, you'll be able to set limits with people in your life so that you're respecting yourself as well as others. You'll be able to say no to the requests of others when you

choose, from your own inner wisdom, to do so, and you'll be able to accept their no when they've chosen to deny your request. You'll also make exceptions to those limits at times when you want to extend yourself for others because they need you, but you won't do this regularly if it means sacrificing your own needs all the time.

* In healthy relationships, you work on taking care of the relationship, but you also work on taking care of yourself.

This isn't an exhaustive list, of course, but these are some of the areas people often struggle with in order to make their relationships healthier and more satisfying.

Reading through this list, did anything pop out at you as problematic in your own relationships? You may have a good idea already of the ways in which your relationships aren't as healthy or balanced as they could be; if so, pat yourself on the back because you're ahead of the game. As you read through this chapter, you'll find some ideas of ways you can begin making changes in this area so that your relationships won't be contributing to your emotional roller coaster on a regular basis. And if you don't have this awareness yet, of course that's okay too—because where we'll be starting is by taking a closer look at some of these areas to help you figure out what you might need to change.

Who's in Your Life Already?

Having a variety of relationships in your life includes family supports (the people in your family you know you can count on and trust), close friends (the people in your life you feel comfortable talking to about at least some of your problems), people you socialize with (people you don't necessarily talk to about private things, but like to get together with to do activities, like going to the movies or shopping), and people you look up to (this could be anyone you feel is a good role model, such as a teacher, a coach, a spiritual leader, or someone who belongs to your Spanish Club at school). Again, this isn't an exhaustive list; the idea is to start you thinking about the people in your life and the variety of relationships you have. Why is this important?

If you don't have many friends in your life, you'll have to rely more on the family or friends you *do* have. This situation can cause a lot of emotional pain for you (for example, how do you feel when you call your one friend and ask her to make plans, but she tells you she's already busy?) and it can take a toll on the people you've become reliant on. The more people you have in your life, the less you have to rely on any one person, and the healthier all those relationships will be. Instead of being devastated that your friend can't spend time with you, you might be disappointed, but you have other people you can call on to go out with instead. The emotional toll will be less for you, and for the other people in your life.

Have you ever noticed times in your life when certain people suddenly start to get on your nerves? That when you spend too much time with them you start to annoy each other? This is usually a sign that you need to take a break from that person, but how do you take a break if you don't have other people in your life to spend time with? And even if this doesn't usually happen for you, what do you do when that one person in your life goes on vacation with her family? Or gets sick? In other words, whom are you going to turn to when she's not available?

Now don't get me wrong: I'm not saying that you can't be self-reliant and that you have to have others in your life to help you through every problem you encounter. But having connections with others is very important to us as human beings, and isolation actually has negative consequences not only for our emotional health but for our physical health as well.

Take some time right now to think about the relationships you currently have. Does it feel as though you have enough people in your life? Do you have people to do social activities and just have fun with? Do you have people you know you can count on and who will support you? Do you have people you can talk to—even if you don't share your deepest, darkest secrets with them, can you let them know you're struggling and trust that they'll be there to help in whatever way they can? Or people you know you can just call to hear the sound of another person's voice, to chat with and to find out how their day went? Think about this honestly, from your wise self.

If you don't believe you have enough people in your life, we'll be addressing this shortly. For now, however, we're going to start with what you've got and look at how to take care of the relationships currently in your life.

Taking Care of Current Relationships

It's very important to nurture your relationships so they don't break down. Think of a relationship as being like a car. You have to take care of big problems, like a rattle in the engine, when they arise, but if you also do regular maintenance on your car, like having the oil changed and the tires rotated, you can often prevent those larger problems from arising. The better

193

care you take of your relationships on a regular basis, the less likely you'll be to have those larger, unexpected problems. The following story demonstrates this idea.

✱ *Andrea's Story*

Andrea and Dana developed such a close relationship when they met in their first year of college that they decided to room together in their second year. In that second year, though, Andrea started to notice changes in her friend. They had both formed some new friendships, and they weren't spending as much time together as they used to, but Dana didn't seem to care as much about their friendship, and Andrea was starting to feel that she was unimportant to her friend. Not wanting to upset Dana, Andrea didn't say anything, and her hurt built up. It seemed to Andrea as though she was always the one reaching out to Dana, and over time, she began to resent how much energy she was putting into the relationship and the fact that she didn't feel as though she was getting much back.

One day, Andrea had had enough; she felt like she was more of an obligation to Dana now and decided she would release Dana from that obligation. So when they got back to school after spring break, Andrea told Dana she was done and that they'd both have to make other living arrangements for the next year. The pair argued, both said some hurtful things, and then they were left in the difficult position of having to live with each other when things were now uncomfortable and tense. The friendship was over.

Andrea let her resentment and hurt build up instead of talking to Dana about these things, and eventually her emotional self took over and ended the friendship, even though that wasn't really what she wanted. It's possible that, if Andrea had addressed the problems at the time by communicating her feelings to Dana, things might have turned out differently. Maybe Dana didn't realize how much her behavior had changed and would have been willing to make an effort to improve the relationship. Or, perhaps the two wouldn't have remained best friends, but by talking about things they might have been able to keep some sort of relationship and not have to live with so much tension. Of course, there's always the possibility that, if Andrea tried to address the problems with Dana, Dana might have exploded and ended the relationship herself, but since the relationship ended anyway, did Andrea really have anything to lose?

Have you ever had relationships end like this? People often allow a relationship to end even though that's not really what they want, rather than acting in effective ways that might save the relationship. Remember: you have to take care of your relationships if you want them to last; if you take them for granted, or if you let your emotions get in the way of acting effectively, you're pretty much guaranteeing the relationship will end in one way or another.

Let's turn now to look at some of the skills that will help you be healthier in your relationships.

Communication Is Key

Communicating assertively with the people in your life is a key part of having healthy relationships. Have you ever found yourself, like Andrea, feeling angry with a friend, but not

195

wanting to talk to her about it because you don't want to rock the boat? Do you ever notice that you have problems expressing your feelings or wants to people you care about because you're afraid they'll get angry with you? So instead you decide to ignore your feelings or (again, like Andrea) to end the relationship, since your friend obviously doesn't care about you that much or she would have noticed there was a problem, right? Wrong! There are lots of things that can go wrong with a relationship when we're not communicating properly.

Let's take a look at the four different ways we communicate. As you're reading through these, think about which styles you act from most often.

* Passive

   If you're a passive communicator, you tend to ignore your emotions rather than express them. You want to keep the peace, and it often feels easier or safer to just avoid your emotions, rather than speak up and risk having the other person feel negatively toward you. But communicating passively means that you disregard your own wants, and over time this will leave you feeling resentful toward the other person because, like Andrea, you're not getting what you want out of the relationship.

* Aggressive

   If you're an aggressive communicator, you express yourself through trying to control others—yelling, swearing, throwing things, making threats, and so on. In other words, you're a bully. You're concerned with getting your own way, and sometimes you don't care about how this affects others. Being aggressive, though, often ends in feelings of guilt and shame for the way you behaved and makes it more likely that you'll lose relationships that were important to you when others decide not to put up with your disrespectful or even abusive behavior.

* Passive-aggressive

  If you're a passive-aggressive communicator, you don't directly express yourself, but you find subtle or back-handed ways of communicating your emotions instead, such as being sarcastic, slamming doors, or giving the silent treatment. You get your message across without actually saying the words, and you do this in a way that's damaging to the relationship.

* Assertive

  If you're an assertive communicator, you express your thoughts, feelings, and opinions in an open, clear, and respectful way. You're concerned with meeting your own needs, as well as the needs of the other person as much as possible through listening and negotiating. Obviously, this is the preferred way of communicating, but it's often one of the most difficult because it means acting from your wise self—and we all know how difficult that can be when emotions become intense!

Reading through these communication styles, were you able to identify which ways you typically use to communicate with others? Keep in mind that you likely use different styles at different times, depending on the person you're interacting with, the situation, and many other factors. The idea here isn't to just label your communication style and fit you into a nice, neat category,

197

but to help you become more aware of how you communicate so that you can make a choice to change that style if you want to.

Of course, it takes time to make changes, so keep in mind that it might be difficult for you to become assertive right away if this isn't how you're used to communicating—like any skill, it needs practice. For some people, acting assertively feels as though they're actually being aggressive, because they're not used to asking for what they want. For many people, learning to be assertive will be uncomfortable and even scary at times, but gradually you'll learn that this is the healthiest way of communicating, and hopefully you'll see positive changes in your relationships. Let's look at some guidelines to help you become more assertive in the way you communicate with others.

How to Be Assertive

Assertiveness is really about acting from your inner wisdom when you're communicating: it's about choosing how to act instead of just reacting from your emotions.

Mindfully Listening to the Other Person

One of the most powerful ways of connecting with another person is by just listening to her. Listening is important in being assertive because when you're asserting yourself you're trying as best you can to meet the needs of the other person as well as your own. So pay attention, and listen to what the other person has to say.

Remembering that mindfulness is doing one thing at a time with your full attention, make sure you're not doing something else while you're talking to the other person—turn off the TV, take out your earbuds, and put your phone away. Send the message that you are paying attention and care about what she has to say. Listen mindfully, with your full attention, noticing when your mind wanders and bringing it back to the present moment; and don't forget acceptance!

Being Nonjudgmental

In chapter 4, we looked at how reducing your judgments will reduce the amount of emotional pain in your life. This skill is also really helpful when it comes to healthy communication. We all know how it feels to be judged: it triggers painful emotions and often gets you stuck in your emotional self. This won't be helpful for you or for the person you're communicating with, so instead of blaming or judging, stick to expressing the facts and your emotions. Remember the golden rule: treat the other person the way you would like to be treated.

Validating

In chapter 5, we looked at self-validation, and how this skill will also reduce your emotional pain. It makes sense, then, that validating the person you're communicating with will have that same soothing effect on that person. And keeping in mind how good it feels for you to be validated by others can help you make this a priority when you're interacting with the people in your life who are important to you.

Validating someone else is very similar to validating yourself. Let the other person know you understand what she feels, but remember, this doesn't necessarily mean you like it or agree with it, just that you get it. In other words, let the other person have her emotions. Reflect back to the other person what she's saying periodically, so that you both know you're understanding her correctly. Sometimes, especially when you know the other person well, you can guess what she might be thinking or feeling in a situation, or you might be able to pick up clues from her facial expression, tone of voice, body language, and so on. When you can point out things that the other person hasn't actually said (for example, "It seems like you're feeling pretty hurt" or "I would imagine you feel really angry about this"), the other person will probably feel as though you really understand and care.

Acting According to Your Morals and Values

Because asserting yourself is about being respectful to yourself and to others, when you're being assertive, it's important to stick to your morals and values. For example, have you ever made up an excuse when someone asked you to do something you didn't want to do? It's perfectly okay to say no, and rather than lie, to just be honest about the reason—even if it's because you simply don't want to! Being assertive means you just tell the person you don't want to do what they're asking of you, and you'll find that your self-respect will increase. Of course, you have to balance this with not damaging the relationship. When the truth is likely to be hurtful and possibly damaging to the relationship, it's okay to create a "little white lie"; for example, by telling your friend you can't come over for dinner because you already have plans, when the truth is that you really don't

200

enjoy her family's style of cooking. Just make sure this doesn't start happening regularly or it will affect your self-respect.

One of the most important things to remember about assertiveness, however, is that even if you act completely skillfully, there are no guarantees that you'll get what you want, although of course it will make it more likely than if you weren't communicating assertively. Ideally you'll reach your goals, but even if you don't, being assertive will ensure that you'll feel good about yourself for acting from your wise self and for maintaining your self-respect and not acting in ways that are damaging to the relationship—and that satisfaction in itself is rewarding!

This next mindfulness exercise is an informal one that you can practice any time you're having an interaction with someone.

Exercise: Communicating Mindfully

Keeping in mind our definition of mindfulness—doing one thing at a time, in the present moment, with your full attention, and with acceptance—be mindful throughout your interaction. So for example, when your mom comes to talk to you about your family's weekend plans, mute the television, put down your cell phone, or close your book. Turn your body toward her. Make eye contact. When you notice your attention wandering from what your mom is saying, gently (without judging yourself) bring yourself back to the conversation; ask her to repeat herself if you missed something. As best as you can, be nonjudgmental about whatever she's telling you, and about any emotions or thoughts that arise within you in response. Don't judge yourself for being distracted; don't judge the distractions; just be aware and notice these things.

201

Because people do tend to notice when you're more present and engaged with them, practicing mindfulness in this way will likely improve your relationships, so bring mindfulness to your interactions—especially with the people you care about—as often as you can.

Having Healthy Limits

In healthy relationships, you also have to work on having healthier limits. Sometimes people get into a pattern of giving or taking all the time; neither is healthy. Remember, balance is key.

Balancing the Give and Take

When you're regularly the giver, you'll usually start to feel resentful at some point because your needs aren't being met and because you're the one putting all the energy into the relationship, even though you're the one who made this choice, at least to begin with. Here's an example.

✱ Kara's Story

Kara was bullied when she was in middle school, and she had very few friends. She looked forward to a new start when she got to high school, and when she met some new people who seemed to like her in the first weeks of school, she decided she'd do everything she could to keep those friends. Because Kara hadn't had many friends, she had spent a lot of her time babysitting and dog-walking, so she had a lot of money saved up. And she found that people seemed to like her even more and want to spend more time with her when she paid for them to go to the movies or to dinner with her, so she was happy to do this.

As time went on, though, and Kara got to know her new friends better, she started to see that it had become an expectation that if they were going out, Kara would pay, and this started to bring up feelings of resentment for her. She felt like she was being used. So Kara decided to try an experiment, and one day when she and her friends went to the movies, she didn't offer to pay. When her friends turned to her at the box office and waited expectantly, Kara felt as though her suspicions were confirmed—her friends were clearly with her only because of her money.

What Kara didn't recognize was that she in fact had trained her friends to expect this behavior from her. Time and again they had gone out together, expecting to pay their own way, but Kara would insist on footing the bill for all of them; so yes, over time, they came to expect this and even take it for granted. This didn't necessarily mean they didn't like Kara or were friends with her only because of her money; it simply meant that Kara had, over time, taught them that whenever they went out together, she paid. If Kara has decided that she doesn't want to be in this position any longer, she needs to use her assertiveness skills and communicate this to her friends. She needs to set a new, healthy limit for herself; for example, that she'll pay for herself but not for her friends, or that she'll pay for everyone and the next time someone else pays, or whatever new rule she decides is more acceptable for her and won't leave her feeling resentful and taken for granted. Then she has to stick to this new limit, essentially retraining her friends.

Can you think of a time when you found yourself in a situation like this? When you felt taken for granted by people in your life, when they seemed to just expect you to do something for them? It could be when you got your driver's license and your best friend expected you to drive her to school every day. Or when your boyfriend came to expect that you would help him with his math homework every weekend because you understand math better than he does. It doesn't feel very good, does it? And that's the other side of this coin—when you're giving all the time, usually you'll start to resent the other person for taking, even if you're the one who made the decision to do the giving in the first place.

How to Set Limits

What many people don't realize is that we train others how to be in relationships with us, just as others train us how to be in relationships with them. This is just part of being human; it's what we learn. So for example, let's say you meet a new person at school and as you get to know her, you see that she likes to tell other people (including you) what to do. If you allow this person to tell you what to do, you're teaching her that her behavior is acceptable to you. If you stop hanging out with her because you don't like the way she's treating you—or if, and this is ideal, you're able to tell her that you don't like it when she tells you what to do—you're teaching her that this behavior isn't okay with you and that she's not allowed to treat you this way. She's just learned what's acceptable for you and what's not, and now she has the choice of changing her behavior (or not).

204

So the idea with having healthy limits is that you need to have "rules" for yourself that are comfortable for you—that are respectful to yourself as well as to others, that match your morals and values, and that result in your being treated the way you want to be treated. When you're not receiving this treatment from others, you communicate it to them when possible, you remove yourself from the situation if possible, or you do your best not to put yourself in that same situation again. In other words, you teach people what's okay for you and what's not, and they then have the choice to continue to be part of your life, given the fact that this is a limit for you. The result will be healthier relationships for you; this will be something that's important for you to keep in mind whether you're working on making your current relationships healthier, as we've been discussing, or whether you're looking to develop new relationships, which we'll look at next.

Increasing Friendships

So far we've been looking at skills that will help you improve your current relationships and make them healthier. But what if you find yourself without many (or any) relationships to work on improving? First, let's take a look at what might be getting in the way of your having relationships.

What Gets in the Way?

While we're all different and have different social needs, as human beings we're social creatures, and we do need other people in our lives. Some people are more content to have a handful of close friends, and others we know as the "social butterflies" who enjoy lots of company. But either way, we're not meant to be alone.

Sometimes, painful emotions—such as anxiety, the most common culprit—get in the way, and people begin to believe (or just want to believe!) that they don't actually need relationships. If this is you, think about this carefully and honestly. These kinds of thoughts are related to your emotional self. If you allow yourself to think about this from your wise self, you will see that somewhere deep down you know that you need—and maybe even want—people in your life. As scary as this can be, it's true.

The bottom line here, though, is that anxiety often prevents you from putting yourself in situations where you could meet people who could become new friends. If this is you, first of all pat yourself on the back for acknowledging it. Then prepare yourself for some hard work, even as you remind yourself that, unless you put the work in, things aren't likely to improve a whole lot. And if you want to survive the emotional roller coaster, this is one obstacle that definitely needs to be tackled.

Thinking of the DBT skills from the perspective of relationships, you might actually want to go back through this book and see how many of the skills we've already looked at can help you with this social anxiety. Mindfulness, for example, will help you reduce your anxiety by being more focused on the present (rather than worrying about what the other person is thinking of you or what will happen if you make a fool of yourself) and more accepting of yourself and your anxiety, which will also reduce your painful emotions. But this is just the start. What about validating your anxiety? Being nonjudgmental toward yourself? And, of course, a biggie: acting opposite to the urge to avoid situations, an urge that usually accompanies anxiety. Hopefully you can see that many, or even all, of the skills we've looked at so far will help you in some way with this, so keep practicing them! Next we're going to look at some tips to help you increase the number of people you have in your life.

Deepening Current Relationships

You've recognized that you don't have enough relationships in your life and you're ready to work on changing this, but how do you do it? I suggest that you start with what's usually most comfortable: the people you already know. Think about the various people you have in your life, from the person who usually sets her mat up beside you in yoga, to the guy who sits next to you and often ends up being your lab partner in science, to the girl you tend to talk to at work when things are slow. Considering the many situations in your life where you're interacting with others, are there people who come to mind with whom you could work on deepening your current relationship? In other words, could you imagine yourself turning to that girl beside you in yoga and starting up a conversation? Or do you think you could bring yourself to say hi to your lab partner when you're walking down the hall at school? Maybe you could ask the girl from work to join you for coffee when you're done with your shift.

The point here is that, for most of us, it's less anxiety provoking and therefore a bit easier to stay within our comfort zone as much as possible. Even though you're still taking a risk, at least you're doing it with someone who is somewhat familiar to you and with whom, presumably, you haven't had any negative interactions—and have probably had at least some small positive interactions.

Remember, too, that you don't have to go big here. I'm not necessarily suggesting you ask your lab partner out on a date! But taking small steps in the direction of developing more of a relationship with people who are already in your life could, just possibly, lead to a new friendship. And even if none of these people turn into actual friends, you'll still be building your self-confidence in this area because you're putting yourself out there and hopefully having positive experiences now and then.

Rekindling Old Friendships

If you can't think of someone already in your life with whom you'd like more of a connection, here's the next thing to think about: is there anyone you used to have a relationship of some sort with and could consider reconnecting with? Before you shut down this possibility, remember that friendships wax and wane. Sometimes you're close to a person, and then for whatever reason you drift apart. This is normal. Even conflict with people in our lives is normal. None of it necessarily means you can't ever go back to having a relationship with a particular person.

So, who is in your life that you could think about reconnecting with? An old friend who moved away or changed schools? Someone you went to dance class with until you moved on to martial arts instead? Someone you were good friends with until a falling-out ended the relationship? Again, this is about taking risks, and I realize that can be frightening. But remember, you're reading this book for a reason—presumably because you've decided to try some new things. So keep an open mind and see what you can do here.

Once you decide on a person, of course, you have to think about the best way of trying to reconnect. You could look her up on Facebook. Or if you can find a phone number, you can actually pick up the phone and call! I know calling tends to be the scarier option, but one thing to remember with e-mails and texts is that there's no human context—no tone of voice, no facial expression or body language—to give the other person any indication of your emotions. There's so much room for misinterpretation, which is why so many misunderstandings happen via electronic communication. I'm not saying you can't communicate this way, of course, but you have to be extra cautious if this is what you choose.

In reaching out to this person, of course, many of the other skills you've learned in this book will come into play. For example, mindfulness: as best as you can, don't catastrophize about how this is going to turn out. Self-validation: it makes sense if you're feeling anxious in this situation! Acting opposite to the urge that anxiety is triggering in you to avoid this situation. And accepting reality as it is: ideally you'll get a positive response, but all you can do is put your best foot forward and hope for the best. Usually, the worst-case scenario is that you don't get what you're asking for. Will you be disappointed if that happens? Probably. But reminding yourself that you're trying new things, acting more skillfully, and trying to improve your life will likely have you still learning something new from that situation. And then you can look at what else you can do to continue moving in this positive direction.

Looking for New Friendships

If you can't think of anyone you might want to deepen your relationship with, and you can't think of anyone you might rekindle a friendship with (or you've tried these options and they haven't worked out), what next? Your last option—and I leave it to last because it's often the most difficult—is to look for new friendships. I say it's often the most difficult because it involves going out of your comfort zone even further and meeting new people. How might you do this?

Well, this involves not just looking for new people but also for new activities, because the only way to meet new people is by putting yourself into new situations. So what can you do that's new? Join a club or sports team, or sign up for an activity at school that will get you interacting with people you don't know; for example, an outdoors club or fundraising committee. Or choose an activity outside of school altogether to get you meeting new people—join a gym or sign up for swimming lessons. Look for some part-time or volunteer work.

Once you get into the new activity, whatever it is, of course you have to put effort into developing new relationships. Think about ways you can break the ice and start talking to people. Of the people you meet, consider who might have the potential to be a friend. And when you do meet someone with potential, think about how you can purposely nurture this possible connection.

You might be surprised at how far a simple smile can go, so do an experiment: Smile at people and notice their reactions. Do they smile back? Do people start talking to you? You might find that, once you've smiled at someone who has smiled back, it tends to happen again the next time you see that person. Notice this. And pay attention to how you feel when you're smiling at others, and when they smile in return.

It's also important to work on accepting that not everyone is going to like you, just as you don't necessarily like everyone you encounter. Accepting this sometimes takes a lot of work, and again goes back to that golden rule—even if you don't like someone, work on treating her the way you would like to be treated. Remembering that people all want to be happy and are trying to be happy as best as they can in this difficult life can help you understand others and their behavior.

Your Next Steps

The focus of this chapter has been on helping you think about the relationships you have with people in your life and learn skills to help you be healthier and more effective in those relationships. Ideally you've already been considering what changes you might need to look at making in this area of your life. And if you haven't, now's the time. Do you have enough relationships? Are they satisfying? Are there any you need to consider ending because they're unhealthy? Or, rather than ending the relationship, are there things you might be able to do to improve them in some way—like setting healthier limits for yourself, or communicating assertively with the other person about what's making you unhappy in the relationship? And, of course, if you don't have enough relationships in your life, to think about steps you might start to take to change this.

Remember, we all need people in our lives; we're all social creatures. And when you have healthier, more satisfying relationships, and you know you have people who care about you and support you when you need it, you'll be more emotionally resilient—in other words, when difficulties arise in your life, as they will, they won't be the catastrophes they've been in the past, and you'll be more able to bounce back from them.

I'm also assuming that you've continued to work on skills from the previous chapters—if you haven't, remember that all these skills take practice, and the work you do with them will pay off in helping you live a happier, healthier life.

Conclusion

When you have difficulties managing your emotions, you find that life often feels unmanageable. Your relationships suffer, and your self-esteem suffers. It's hard to succeed in school and to work toward goals, and sometimes even just to think straight. The skills you've learned in this book can help you change all that. If you've been working hard on putting them into practice, it's likely that you've seen some changes, although they might only be small ones right now. The longer you continue practicing these skills, though, the more positive changes you'll see.

Of course it's not easy, and you really need to develop the mindset that these skills are a new way of living your life. You can't just read this book and expect changes to miraculously occur—it's up to you to put the skills into practice and to work on changing the way you've been living your life. If you can make that commitment to yourself, though, practicing skills even when things are difficult and you know it would much easier to just allow yourself to fall back into old habits, you'll learn over time to manage your emotions in a healthier way. In this final section I want to help you generate some ideas about how you can continue to do the work you've started to make those positive changes.

Making a Plan

First, take some time to think about what you might do differently that will help you make these changes. For example, you might need to work your way through this book a second time, going more slowly, practicing the skills more as you go along. Sometimes people read through books like these too quickly, without putting as much effort into practice as they could have, and the result is that they don't absorb the material the way they need to in order to incorporate the skills into their lives. Going through this book too quickly can also cause you to feel overwhelmed by the amount you're learning. So take it one step at a time. Even if you have to spend a couple of months focusing on just one skill, do what you need to do in order to learn the material and make helpful and healthy changes in your life.

As with anything in life, writing out a plan can make this a little easier. Read through the following questions and ideas to help you come up with a plan. You might want to make some notes about this on a blank piece of paper.

* What changes, if any, have you started making since you began reading this book? For example, have you started practicing mindfulness exercises? Have you been noticing more often when you're being controlled by your emotional or reasoning self as opposed to acting from your wise self? Or have you been working on communicating more effectively with people in order to improve your relationships?

* If you haven't started making any changes yet, can you think of what's gotten in the way? What's preventing you from doing the work? Are you afraid? Are you undecided about whether these skills will actually help? If these kinds of thoughts are holding you back, remind yourself that what you've been doing so far hasn't been working; you need to make some kind of changes, so why not start here? If you can think of anything else that's getting in the way, see if you can work around it. Ask friends and family for help if you can't figure this out on your own.

* Take some time to review the chapters in this book, and see if you can identify one area you could start working on; for example, you might have a situation currently happening in your life that you really want to be effective in. Or you might start working on taking better care of yourself with self-soothing activities. It's usually not a great idea to start with a skill that's going to be really difficult for you, so try to choose something that seems doable, even if it's not necessarily what you would think of as the most important area for you to start on. If you can start with something a little less difficult and have some small successes, it will make you more likely to continue working on skills in areas that are more difficult for you over time.

Cheerleading Yourself!

Remembering that the way you're thinking and talking to yourself will have an impact on your feelings and behaviors, notice how you're talking to yourself about the changes you're trying to make. Rather than focusing on how difficult it is to make changes, or how much energy it takes, and instead of pointing out to yourself when you don't achieve a goal, cheerlead yourself. You might even want to write out a list of encouraging statements that you can read to yourself at times when you're struggling; for example, "Yes, this is hard, and as long as I keep working at it, I'll get there" or "Using these new skills really takes a lot of effort, but I've seen some small changes, so I think it'll be worth it in the long run."

Asking for Help

Asking for help is not a sign of weakness—actually, it takes courage. And I'm sure that the people who care about you will not only be happy to help if you ask them to, but also be happy to know that you're working on helping yourself manage your emotions more effectively. These skills are going to benefit the people who care about you as well, so lend them this book or teach them a specific skill you're struggling with, and let them know exactly what you'd like them to do to help you (for example, pointing out when you're being judgmental or when you're acting from your emotional self). Keep in mind, though, that if you ask for help, you have to then be willing to accept the help that's offered—so do your best to act from your wise self and not get angry with your family or friends when they're doing what you've asked them to!

Being Patient

Changing the way you deal (or don't deal!) with your emotions is a long road. You've been stuck in this pattern for a lifetime, so you have to remind yourself that you won't be able to make these changes overnight. As hard as it is, have patience and be kind with yourself. I can tell you from my own experience that if you put the effort into practicing these skills, over time, you will see some kind of positive change. Some people see changes sooner than others, and everyone is different.

Remember the inspirational Dr. Linehan, who not only created this treatment but also used these skills in order to heal herself. If you work at it, you can make your life a happier, healthier one. I wish you luck on your journey.

Sheri Van Dijk, MSW, is a mental health therapist and renowned dialectical behavior therapy (DBT) expert. She is author of seven books, including *Calming the Emotional Storm, Don't Let Your Emotions Run Your Life for Teens,* and *Relationship Skills 101 for Teens.* Her books focus on using DBT skills to help people manage their emotions and cultivate lasting wellbeing. She is also the recipient of the R.O. Jones Award from the Canadian Psychiatric Association.

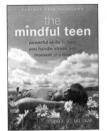

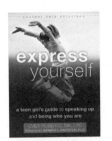

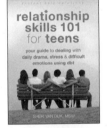